Praise for
Teaching Peace

"*Teaching Peace* is a straightforward, clear approach to one of the most important issues in the violence prevention arena—the struggle to teach our youth respect and understanding for others in a country suffering from divisions along the lines of race, gender, class, and age. . . . The guide gives the reader a firm grasp of the social issues that affect and sometimes promote bias and prejudice in the U.S. and provides a solid foundation necessary to understand and teach our nation's youth peace, tolerance, and appreciation for all people."

—DEBORAH PROTHROW-STITH, M.D.,
Community Violence Prevention Project, Harvard School of Public Health

"A practical handbook for peace activists in all walks of life . . . excitingly instructive and inspiring."

—PAUL L. ADAMS, M.D., Visiting Professor of Child & Adolescent Psychiatry, University of Tennessee Center for Health Services, Memphis; Professor Emeritus of Psychiatry, University of Texas Medical Branch, Galveston

TEACHING PEACE

How to Raise Children
to Live in Harmony—
Without Fear, Without Prejudice,
Without Violence

Jan Arnow

A PERIGEE BOOK

A Perigee Book
published by
The Berkley Publishing Group
200 Madison Avenue
New York, NY 10016

Copyright © 1995 by Jan Arnow

Book design by Irving Perkins Associates

Cover design by Wendy Bass

Cover illustration by The Stock Market, copyright © 1990 by David Woods.

First edition: October 1995

Published simultaneously in Canada.

Library of Congress Cataloging-in-Publication Data

Arnow, Jan, date.
   Teaching peace : how to raise children to live in harmony : without
prejudice, without fear, without violence / Jan Arnow.
     p. cm.
   "A Perigee Book."—T.p.
   ISBN 0-399-52155-0 (pbk.)
   1. Child rearing—United States. 2. Prejudices in children—United
States—Prevention. 3. Prejudices—Study and teaching—United
States. 4. Violence in children—United States—Prevention.
I. Title.
HQ769.A764   1995
649'.1—dc20   95-8712
                                                    CIP

Printed in the United States of America

10 9 8 7 6 5 4 3 2 1

For all children,
including my own: Sam, Chloe, and Abraham Hawkins

Contents

Acknowledgments   ix
Introduction   xi

Part One
THE HOME

ONE   Conditioning for Hatred and Violence   3
           War Toys   4
           Video Games   7
           Television   12
           The Next Step: Real Violence   20
           Media Literacy   22
           Responding to Kids' Concerns   25
TWO   Evaluating Your Child's Literature   44
           Sexism   46
           Racism   54

Part Two
HOME TO SCHOOL

THREE   The School Climate:
           Creating a Supportive Setting   69
               Who Fails and Who Succeeds?   71

	Why Keep Kids in School?	72
	Strategies to Improve School Culture	77
FOUR	Growing Up Equal:	
	Gender Fairness in the Classroom	111
	Early Gender Socialization	111
	Sexism in the School	113
	Sexual Harassment	118
	The Call for Equity	121
FIVE	Parents and Teachers as Partners	140
	Barriers to Parent Participation	141
	Redefining the Concept	144

Part Three
HOME TO SCHOOL TO COMMUNITY

SIX	Multiculturalism and Your Community	161
	Persistence of Social Problems	162
	Hate Crimes and Gangs	163
	Community Services	170
	Communicating Across Cultures	174
SEVEN	Actions as Antidotes: Working for Change	183
	Compassion Fatigue	184
	Reactions to Troubled Times	186
	Commitment to Change	188
EIGHT	Our Universal Challenge	205
	Resources	215
	Keywords	226
	Bibliography	229

Acknowledgments

As with most projects of this scope, this book would not have been possible without the help and encouragement of many people.

To the following scholars, authorities, colleagues and friends, I offer my profound respect and sincerest appreciation:

Joe Argabrite, my friends at the Kentucky Department of Education, Carol Besse, Michael Boggs, Miranda Boggs, Bill Butler, my two- and four-legged friends in the Cherokee Canine Club, the C.I.S. Professional Women's Group, Martha Neal and Graham Cooke, Lorraine Doss, Tom Hanley and the crew at the Eastern Stream Center on Resources and Training, Ronni Lundy, Elizabeth King, John Knowles, Baylor Landrum III, Charles Mays, John McLaughlin, Al Needlman, Roz Parnis, Gary Peschka, Nancy Peterson and the Edenside Gallery, C.J. Pressma and the whole TriMedia Interactive group, the Ramos family, Lydia Reid, Zan Sawyer-Dailey, Pat Ross, Linda Scholle Cowan, Julie Segal, Debbie Shannon, Jeff Smith, Tommy Smith, Vertner Smith, John and Kim Stone, Hollie Thacker and Bob Zeitner.

In addition, to the following people I offer a special thank-you:

Julie Merberg, my editor at Perigee, for the freedom to pursue this project, and for her vision, enthusiasm and encouragement along the way;

Stewart Callner, my brother, for believing in me uncondition-
   ally;

Rush Limbaugh and all of the other neo-conservative talk
   show hosts, for making "multiculturalism" a household
   word;

The very special group who publicly expressed their dedication to the issues several years ago with their participation
   in the making of the album " 'Til Their Eyes Shine," and the
   film "Child of Mine, the Lullaby Video": Karla Bonoff, Jim
   and Ginger Brown and Carol Ross of the Ginger Group,
   Mary-Chapin Carpenter, Rosanne Cash, Brenda Derrane,
   Don DeVito, Gloria Estefan, Gerry Goffin, G. Gruska, Em-
   mylou Harris, John Ingrassia, Carol King, Kate and Anna
   McGarrigle, Laura Nyro, Maura O'Connell, Brenda Russell,
   E. Shipley, David Waldman, Dionne Warwick and Deniece
   Williams;

All of my friends who found that asking the simple question,
   "Is there anything I can do to help?" provided them with
   ample opportunities to make phone calls, check facts, review the manuscript and other sundry chores: Paul Adams,
   Maureen Cravens, Barb Disborough, Amanda Lichtenstein,
   Cam Hagan, Abraham Hawkins, Chloe Hawkins, Sam Hawkins, Jim Doubtfire Oakes, Deborah Ossofsky, Dean Pear-
   son and Tom Thacker. A very special thanks to Steve Doss,
   who showed up day after day to do whatever needed to be
   done, and to Steve Weller, without whom I would still be
   lost in cyberspace;

Barbara Sparky West, for always being ready to go wherever
   I needed to go;

And Gloria Needlman, one of the best early childhood educators of all times, who taught me the meaning of human
   rights.

Introduction

Suppose we wanted to design a training program in which the primary objective was to prepare children to hate by the time they entered kindergarten. What would that program be like? Perhaps there would be:

- free access to toys and games where your ability to win depends on your ability to maim and kill,
- the equivalent of 22 days of classroom instruction per year just spent on advertising those toys and games,
- an increase in the sales of war toys of over 700 percent within the most recent decade,
- an overexposure to video games in which the object is to solve conflicts and gain power through the use of violence,
- unrestricted access to comic books with names like Asylum, Bloodshot, Death Mask, Doom and Necroscope, all with a preponderance of anti-heroes,
- easy access to drugs of all kinds, coupled with decreasing funding for drug intervention and prevention,
- as many as 25 percent of the children who shoot people high on alcohol or drugs like crack or PCP, all of which are "disinhibitors" that may spur violent behavior,
- disputes settled with guns rather than fists or words,

- more than 200 million guns in the hands of ordinary citizens,
- access to these weapons by children, with more than 135,000 children bringing guns to school each day and nearly two dozen teens and adults killed every day by firearms,
- shootings or hostage situations in schools occurring in at least 35 states and the District of Columbia,
- twice as much time spent watching TV (22,000 hours) as time spent in the classroom by age 18 (11,000 hours),
- only 10 percent of children's viewing time spent watching children's television; the other 90 percent spent watching programs designed for adults,
- twenty-six violent acts per hour depicted on television,
- at least 3.3 million children at risk for witnessing parental abuse each year; these children would witness the range of abusive behavior from hitting, punching or slapping to fatal assaults with guns and knives.

Perhaps we're already well under way if our aim is to prepare children to hate.

When I lecture and conduct workshops for teachers, parents, corporations and community leaders throughout the country, I often begin with this exercise. After citing the statistics, I then ask, "What's wrong with this picture?" Of course, the answer is that these statistics are all appallingly current, and such a program to teach children to hate, designed around these very elements, already exists. We live it each day, in every part of this country, at every socioeconomic level. And yet we wonder why our children have grown so violent and so hateful.

One conflict leads to another. Studies have shown that if children learn that violence, conflict and hatred are the prevailing options, these behaviors become normal to them and they are more than likely to perpetuate them into their adult lives. To me, this is a frightening reality. It means that no matter how much effort and resources we pour into ending neighborhood and world conflicts today, there are several generations waiting in the wings to begin further conflicts tomorrow, generations of children who are already trained and more than willing—and in many cases, eager—to participate.

I am not satisfied with this vision of the future. As an educator, a concerned citizen and a mother of three, I have written this book for others who may also be apprehensive about tomorrow.

The views that I express and the suggestions that I make have grown out of several basic premises that I hold:

- The 21st century is now almost five years away. To help us predict how America will fare in the new century, we must pay very close attention to some very important demographic changes: the shift in the age structure and diversity of our population; the growing population of "at-risk" children and adults; the significant transfer of resources away from our children and young families to our mature work force and aging population; and the government policy of increasingly doing less to ensure a competitive and productive future for our children.

- By the middle of the new century, our world will be run by those who are children today. But the decisions that will affect them before they're old enough to assume leadership will be made by us. As we wonder what kind of leaders they will be, based on the powerful forces of violence and hatred with which they are faced, we must remember that we are in charge today. We have the choice of either passing on to them a legacy of sustainable coexistence, or relinquishing our considerable power and allowing the crisis of violence to increase its own destructive momentum.

- Caring for children is not just the responsibility of parents, nor is education solely the job of school systems. Everyone raises children, regardless of whether or not we have children of our own. It is, therefore, everyone's job to address the issues in this book.

- There is no absolute truth. Each of us must search within ourselves for that which is meaningful and true to us, and the search must be ongoing. Because change is a constant, we cannot be satisfied tomorrow with what we decided today. Similarly, what is effective for one person in one situation may not be so for another in a different situation. It is absolutely normal to have conflicting feelings about the issues covered in this book. The debate will continue and the struggle for clarity on these issues will go on. But in the meantime, parents must parent and teachers must teach. What is important is not that all people agree on all issues and all truths, but that we continue to explore options and present ourselves as thoughtful, humane role models to our children.

- If we begin with compassion, all activities become positive experiences.

The problems discussed in *Teaching Peace* have taken generations to attain the position they hold in our lives today. They will not be eliminated, or even addressed sufficiently, in a sound bite. In fact, we may never see in our lifetimes the results that we want. But that is *not* a reason to put off addressing the issues in positive ways. It is in this spirit that I welcome each of you to the pages of this book. I offer it to you in acknowledgment of our similarities, our differences, and the common bond we have in believing that children, all children, deserve a peaceful future.

"If we are to reach real peace in the world we shall have to begin with the children; and if they will grow up in their natural innocence, we won't have to struggle; we won't have to pass fruitless ideal resolutions, but we shall go from love to love and peace to peace, until at last all the corners of the world are covered with that peace and love for which consciously or unconsciously the whole world is hungering."

MOHANDAS KARAMCHAND (MAHATMA) GANDHI

PART ONE

The Home

CHAPTER ONE

Conditioning for Hatred and Violence

Play is the way children practice for the adult world. Anyone who has watched a small child playing with a simple wooden airplane knows how a toy can stimulate a child's imagination. Toys and games are the turnstile through which the child passes to enter the adult world. Playtime should be a magical juncture during which children can feel strong and empowered. When they play, children should be able to work on their understanding of the difference between make-believe and reality; they should begin to comprehend and process basic ideas about morals and values; and they should be learning about cooperation and the needs of others.

Increasingly, however, as toys of aggression, conflict and war proliferate, playtime is beginning to resemble more a tour of duty than a series of magic moments.

Consider this:

- Nineteen million toy guns were sold in the United States in 1986. A year later that number jumped 73.7 percent to 33 million sold.
- Sales of war toys have risen over 500 percent from 1986 to 1990, to well over a billion dollars a year.

■ Despite the fact that the winter holiday season celebrates
life and light, in the past decade more than half of the best-
selling toys and games during that season have been various
types of war toys.

Violence in our society is at an all-time high, and children are
increasingly involved as active participants. Children's toys, it
seems, are teaching them that war and killing are perfectly acceptable methods of dealing with conflict.

WAR TOYS

War toys are playthings which are used to solve conflict, gain
power or win through the use of violence. The aim of a war toy
is to wound or kill. While it is true that war play has been with
us for centuries (remnants of what might be war toys have been
found that date back to the Middle Ages), what has changed over
time is as important as what has remained the same.

The Influence of Advertising

In the past, children were the directors of their own play experiences, selecting both the essence and inventory of their recreational activities. But for the last several decades, and especially
since the introduction of the *Star Wars* toys in the 1970s, children have been channeled into using single-purpose, character-
specific toys to reenact scenes they've seen in the movies and on
television. The media and toy industries began to determine the
content of children's play, the characters of choice and the les-
sons they were supposed to learn from them.

By removing all restrictions that protected children from commercial exploitation, the deregulation of children's television in

the 1980s was another major force in changing the shape of children's play. The resulting collaboration between television producers and toy manufacturers created a rich opportunity for product-driven shows such as *Adventures of the Power Rangers* to clog the airwaves with programs touted as entertainment for children. But since young children have a difficult time discerning the difference between advertising and programming, these shows became what we can consider the first infomercials, dictating toy choices to children at an alarming rate. This program format quickly became the norm in children's television. A proliferation of war toy lines flooded the market, almost all directly tied to violent cartoon characters. Children now had detailed daily instruction on what toys to buy and how to play with them. Playtime changed dramatically.

Whereas children once played outside, interacted with others and used their fertile imaginations to engage in their rich fantasy lives, they now sat glued in front of the television set, passively fed information on what to buy and how to use it. The locus of control had been taken away from the child and placed firmly in the hands of adult toy manufacturers whose bottom line was dependent on how big a share they could gain from the lucrative juvenile market. The most profound effect deregulation and the resulting advertising blitz had on children was to create the need in them to own very specific toys, many of them toys of aggression and violence, simply in order to play.

We shouldn't be surprised that children seem to be obsessed with violence.

Toy Guns and Dolls

The most dramatic increase in war toy sales has been the rising sale of toy guns. Despite the annual count of tragedies involving children and teens whose toy guns are mistaken for the real thing by adults with real guns, toy designers are sinking to new depths to come up with novel gimmicks for toy guns to make them more realistic and exciting. Some of them are called "replicas" or "imitations" because they so closely resemble real weapons. A quick stroll down the toy gun aisle of your local toy store will reveal a frightening variety of options for children today.

Marketed in tandem with many of these weapons are the replicas of the characters who use them in the cartoons and advertisements, already named and with their personalities and functions clearly defined. These dolls are equipped for the nineties, linked with provisions, or what the Army currently calls "organic assets," that would rival any nation's armed forces: attack vehicles, artillery lasers and missile systems.

As if the violent nature of these characters and their accoutrements weren't enough, they frequently portray racial and sexual stereotypes promoting hatred in our society—able-bodied white men as the heroes, foreign-born males, some with disabilities, as the evil characters, women as victims—setting children up for dangerous prejudices and bigotry later on in life.

The growing realism of these toys is playing an increasingly important role in children's play. They reinforce negative, aggressive behavior, especially when supported by exposure to violence on television and at the movies. These toys are teaching our children that:

- people who look and act differently should be defeated;
- possession of weapons is acceptable;
- killing and other forms of violence are acceptable ways of dealing with conflict; and
- people do not suffer or really die as a result of war and conflict.

Each time we purchase these toys for our children, or allow others to give them to our children as gifts, we communicate our tacit approval of the toys and the violent behavior they inspire.

VIDEO GAMES

The child's room is dark except for the eerie glow of the television. The child sits staring at the screen for hours on end, his body frozen, tense from the pumping adrenaline. Only his hands move, jerking to stab at the joystick and buttons on a small black box. Periodically he emits sounds—a growl, a grunt, an anguished moan. He is deeply engrossed in a video game.

If you are a parent or care giver of a child in the nineties, this scene is probably quite familiar to you. You aren't alone. One in every three homes in America now has a video game unit of some kind. Add to this the colossal number of handheld video game units sold in the last decade and the fact that every shopping mall and movie theater is electric with arcade versions of the games, and you can see that we have created a situation in which no child in America, rural or urban, rich or poor, is far away from a video game fix.

Video games were the first medium to offer a child the opportunity to interact with the moving, visual images on the television screen. They began the expansion of the small screen entertainment industry into our children's lives, and continue to play a major role. Among the many reasons for the enormous interest and fondness children have shown for video games are these:

- Children can elevate their skill level over a relatively short period of time with little physical effort. Compared to most sports or other activities, such as learning to play a musical instrument, the skills to master most video games are acquired at lightning speed.

- The games themselves can be programmed to match the player's skill level as he moves up through levels of difficulty, allowing incremental adjustment of the challenges.
- Video games offer a substitute world in which to operate, away from the stresses of interaction with parents, school and peers.
- Children can enter into the lives of their favorite characters on the screen and take action as those characters, activating the dormant medium of television and giving them a sense of omnipotence and control.

While we can understand the appeal of these games for our children, we can't help but wonder what a steady diet of these games is doing to their physical, mental and emotional development.

Violence

From the very first appearance of computerized arcade games, there have been questions about the level of violence in such games. Not only are violence and aggression pervasive themes in most video games, but also a child's ability to win is in direct proportion to his ability to maim and kill. In a study by the National Coalition on Television Violence, which surveyed the ninety-five most popular video games, 58 percent of them were games of warfare and 83 percent featured violent themes. There are only two real choices in these games—kill or die—and violence is the only guideline by which the players function.

Despite the clusters of children often seen hovering around an arcade game or in front of a television that is hooked by an umbilicus to a Nintendo set, there are rarely team players among them. Proximity, in this case, does not equal community. Typically, an autonomous individual, acting alone, performs an aggressive act against a screen enemy. As a bonus, the advances of modern technology have made possible a frightening degree of realism in which to play out these deadly scenarios, by digitizing the movements of real actors playing the parts of the characters.

Because the societies depicted in most of these games are hierarchical, the player must destroy the other characters in a "winner takes all" scheme in order to advance through the various levels of the society and game. This creates another problem with serious social consequences: Rather than learning and using skills of negotiation and mediation to move forward, children learn to shoot first and talk later, if at all. Again, many of the enemy characters

STRAIGHT TALK

"Our children are growing up today in an ethically polluted nation where instant sex without responsibility, instant gratification without effort, instant solutions without sacrifice, getting rather than giving, and hoarding rather than sharing are the too-frequent signals of our mass media, popular culture, business, and political life . . . Nowhere is the paralysis of public and private conscience more evident than in the neglect and abandonment of millions of our shrinking pool of children, whose future will determine our nation's ability to compete and lead in a new era."

MARION WRIGHT EDELMAN,
President,
Children's Defense Fund

in these games are not Americans but foreigners, training our children to accept conflict and violence against people who are different from them.

Even while our schools and neighborhoods are rapidly becoming diverse, we are conditioning our children to have less tolerance for differences, and are legitimizing the violence against one another by our unspoken agreement to allow them to play with these games.

Gender Bashing

Another complicated aspect of video violence is that game producers know that their audience is 75 percent male and they cater to that segment of the market. The active characters in most games are male, while the most prevalent roles for female characters are those of victims. The covers of the fifty most popular video games show an overwhelming imbalance between men and women—115 male and 9 female characters, a ratio of 13 to 1. When women are included in these games, they are usually acted upon rather than being the initiators of action.

Sex bias and gender stereotyping in video games, as in other media, has stunning implications for both boys and girls. Children learn that girls are weak and dependent, and constantly in need of assistance, conditioning boys to assume dominant gender roles. In addition, because childrens' interest in computers begins with games, the fact that the most popular video games are more appealing to boys than to girls contributes to the continuing imbalance of males in the computer industry and other fields requiring technological skills.

Immediate Gratification

Having a "long attention span" means simply having the ability to distinguish between areas of stimulation, to prioritize them, and then to focus on the most important ones. Children begin to gain this ability fairly early on, learning to wait their turn and to suppress their need for immediate gratification. But those who spend time playing video games on a regular basis have a greater delay in the development of their focusing ability. Because video games appeal to short-term, impulsive thinking rather than longer-term, critical thinking, they can create an alteration in a child's sense of time, producing an inability to sustain attention. Many parents and teachers have found that they must condense their instructions so that they come to the point much more quickly in order to keep video-bred children attentive. We are producing a generation of children who will not be able to sustain their attention for longer than the amount of time it takes them to laserize and obliterate their enemy on a television screen.

Our Challenge

The small screen, whether on a television set, a home computer or an arcade game, has become universally accepted as the information-delivery system of choice. School systems all over the country are allocating major funding for computer-assisted learning centers, and the sale of home computer game units is soaring. Yet how much do we really know about what our children are exposed to through these games? What are the rationalizations we have made to one another in order to allow this medium to flourish?

The argument that these violent and bloody video games are appropriate outlets for adolescent aggression is faulty. Most research shows that playing these games supports and sometimes spurs violent activity. The belief that the fantasy world in video games bears little or no resemblance to real life is inaccurate. Some of the most popular games depict inner-city police officers shooting drug dealers, and street gangs rivaling one another, effectively functioning as instruction manuals for insuring particular responses in similar real-life situations.

TELEVISION

Boob tube. TV. Idiot box. Whatever we choose to call it, television is omnipotent and powerful. It has the capacity to entertain us, inform us, shrink the world around us and tell us where to shop, what to buy and how to act. As such, television has surpassed all other forms of media to become the primary tool for mass communications. With more than 98 percent of all homes in the United States equipped with at least one set, television is, perhaps, our strongest socializing agent, and its programming helps shape our personalities, attitudes and perceptions of reality.

For some, television is a bastion of free speech, sacrosanct and untouchable. But for others, the very thought of television's pervasiveness and power raises a red flag, especially when it comes to the content of television programming and its effects on children. What children see, they imitate. And what they see on both broadcast and cable television is violence, real and simulated.

The debate about curbing television violence is not new. What *has* changed over the years is the degree to which violence has become standard fare. When Congress first investigated the issue in the 1950s, 16 percent of prime time programs featured violence and crime. By 1961 the figure had increased to 50 percent. And by 1990, although thousands of reports had been conducted showing the detrimental effects of the proliferation of violence on television, nearly 80 percent of prime time shows broadcast at least one overt threat to hurt or kill a person.

STRAIGHT TALK

"We cannot condone children being exposed to a steady diet of TV violence any more than we can condone teaching of violence in our schools."

ARNOLD FEGE,
spokesperson for National PTA

The accumulated research of nearly three thousand studies indicates a strong correlation between the viewing of violent images and aggressive behavior. What's more, evidence has been mounting that children's exposure to violence on television has long-lasting effects on their behavior.

The impact of television on children is most easily understood within the context of normal child development. All infants have the capacity and desire to imitate adult human behavior, an instinct evidenced by their frequent mirroring of adult facial expressions. Children as young as fourteen months of age have been found to exhibit behaviors that they have seen on television.

Up to age three or four, many children are not fully able to distinguish reality from fantasy on television programs. Their grasp of motives for the behavior of characters on television and the subtleties of the moral conflicts in which they engage is not

well developed. Studies have shown that children believe,
for example, that Sesame Street really does exist; that the characters on television can see and hear us; and that what they see
on the screen is actually inside the set. In their minds, the world of television is entirely factual, and while they may learn differently as they grow older, these earliest impressions remain with them—images of violence as an exciting, swift and effective way to solve conflicts, unencumbered by any inherent long-term consequences of pain or tragedy.

STRAIGHT TALK

"Television violence affects youngsters of all ages, of both genders, at all socioeconomic levels and all levels of intelligence. The effect is not limited to children who are already disposed to being aggressive and is not restricted to this country."

DRS. LEONARD ERON AND
ROWELL HUESMANN,
testifying before Congress in 1992

Effects of Violence

An eleven-year-old boy in Alabama shot his pal in the neck with a .22-caliber rifle, mimicking a television commercial for a child's game with guns. A seven-year-old Oklahoma boy hung himself after watching a cartoon where hanging was depicted. A five-year-old child set his trailer home on fire after watching an MTV segment featuring Beavis and Butt-Head extolling the glories of setting things on fire. That blaze killed his three-year-old sister. The causal link between children's exposure to television violence and their propensity to engage in violent behavior is no longer conjecture. Life is beginning to imitate art with increasing frequency.

A variety of effects has been associated with repeated viewing of television violence:

- *Increased aggression*
  Viewing TV violence increases the likelihood that children will use violence against their friends, and it increases the severity of the violence they will use.
- *Desensitization*
  Viewing television violence decreases in children feelings of sensitivity to the pain and suffering of others. In the opinion of Dr. William H. Dietz, Jr., chair of the American Academy of Pediatrics' Task Force on Children's Television, children who are exposed to a lot of televised violence seem to become deadened to gore. "If you are desensitized to violence," Dietz says, "your feelings about blowing somebody away on a subway are less likely to be tinged by remorse." Children also become less concerned about the aggressive actions of other children, sometimes developing a "bystander" mentality in which real violence is viewed as unreal.
- *Fearfulness*
  Children who watch a lot of televised violence feel the world around them is a more dangerous place than those who don't watch much television. The American Psychological Association suggests that with increased viewing, exposure to media violence increases fearfulness about becoming a victim of violence and may compound some children's natural anxieties.

Other, more subtle effects have also been found:

- *Decrease in the sensation of danger*
  Viewing TV violence can remove or reduce inhibitions that would normally preclude aggressive behavior.

■ *Reinforcement of cultural stereotypes*

Much of commercial television, violent or not, reinforces familiar stereotypes, presenting exaggerated or extremely narrow representations of people and their activities that may give children distorted opinions about the world. Studies have made it clear that heavy viewing of action shows by eight- to ten-year-old children leads them to develop negative images of blacks, for example, viewing them as less competent and less obedient to the law than whites. Women are often in need of rescue, and seem incapable of defending or helping themselves. Single women are likely to be attractive, and they are often victims of violence in the first fifteen minutes of an adventure show. Girls who watch more game shows and fantasy-action shows accept the stereotypes of women as less competent than men and in general show more prejudice against their own sex.

■ *Domestic violence*

Viewing violence on television can contribute to later domestic violence. Dr. Judith Reisman, in her 1991 book, *Soft Porn Plays Hardball*, states that if a young man becomes sexually excited while watching a young woman, and that young woman is brutally attacked, the violence becomes added to the erotic repertoire in the young man's imagination.

■ *Unreality about conflicts*

Children who watch television can be misled because most programming makes it appear that there is, or at least ought to be, an easy solution to every problem they encounter. Also, by depicting most conflicts as resolved in no more than thirty or sixty minutes, television viewing can greatly reduce a child's attention span and capacity for dealing with adversity and conflict on a protracted basis.

The long-term effects are no more promising. In a twenty-two-year study conducted in upstate New York, Dr. Leonard D. Eron discovered that the more children watched television at age eight, the more serious were the crimes they were convicted of by age thirty *and* the harsher the punishment they inflicted on their own children. Dr. Eron believes that what one learns about life from the television screen is transmitted even to the next generation. Whether watching children's cartoon programming (where the increase in violent actions jumped fourfold after deregulation in the 1980s) or the nightly news, the indication is clear that childhood television viewing is becoming a better predictor of teenage and adult aggression than social class, child-rearing practices and a host of other factors.

STRAIGHT TALK

"Your delegates to the United Nations are not as important as the people in this room [broadcasters]. We are the ones that determine what the people's attitudes are. It's in our hands."

TED TURNER,
AFA Journal,
October 1989

Though it is natural and easy to blame the marketplace—the television and advertising industries—for the dismal state of programming today, we have to remember that ultimately, the marketplace is not the raging avaricious entity that it is often depicted as being; it is neutral. The market is us. And with advertisers spending as much as $500 million annually to reach us, we need to do as Martha Bayles, a former television critic for the *Wall*

Street Journal, suggests: Stop using a constant (the profit motive) to explain a variable (the amount of violence in the media). Instead, use another variable—namely, the deeper cultural changes that have occurred over the past several decades.

DID YOU KNOW?

- In 1973, when a town in Canada was wired for television signals, University of British Columbia researchers observed first- and second-graders, and within two years, the incidence of hitting, biting and shoving increased 160 percent in those classes.
- After TV deregulation in the early 1980s, the average number of violent acts depicted on television increased from eighteen to twenty-six per hour. (Source: National Association for the Education of Young Children.)
- The rate of violence in children's programming is three times the rate in prime time TV shows. (Source: University of Pennsylvania Annenberg School of Communication.)
- Only 10 percent of children's viewing time is spent watching children's television. The other 90 percent is spent watching programs designed for adults. (Source: National Association for the Education of Young Children.)
- Crime is portrayed on television about fifty-five times more often than it occurs in real life. (Source: University of Pennsylvania Annenberg School of Communication.)
- There are five to six violent acts per hour on television during prime time; there are nearly three times that

(continued)

amount on Saturday morning children's programs. Even more graphic violence, sexual content and mature themes are accessible in the 60 percent of homes that have cable TV and VCRs (Source: American Psychological Association.)

- 98 percent of American homes have at least one television which is watched each week for an average of twenty-eight hours by two- to eleven-year-olds and twenty-three hours by teenagers. (Sources: American Psychological Association and A.C. Nielsen Company.)

- A child who watches an average of two to four hours of television a day will have witnessed 8,000 homicides and 100,000 other acts of violence by the time he reaches junior high school, and 40,000 killings and 200,000 acts of violence by the time he is eighteen. (Source: American Psychological Association.)

- In the United States, children spend more time in front of the television than in front of a teacher. Even children at the lower end of the TV-use spectrum—2.5 hours of viewing per day—will have spent more time in front of a television by the time they are eighteen (22,000 hours) than in the classroom (11,000 hours), and will be viewing an average of 5 violent acts per hour of prime time and 26.4 violent acts per hour of children's programming. (Sources: Children and Non-Violence and Edell Health Letter.)

- Viewing violence in the mass media has long-lasting consequences. Viewing violence increases the fear of becoming a victim, increases desensitization to violence and increases viewers' appetites for becoming involved with violence. (Source: American Psychological Association.)

THE NEXT STEP: REAL VIOLENCE

Our children are our future—but the decline in youth well-being on a variety of indicators leads us to question the value of that future. Consider these statistics:

- The chance that a teenager will die a violent death (by accident, murder or suicide) increased 12 percent from 1984 to 1988. (Source: the Center for the Study of Social Policy, Washington, DC.)
- Of 535 elementary schoolchildren living in Chicago's south side, 26 percent had seen someone shot and 29 percent had seen a stabbing. (Source: Children's Defense Fund.)
- One in six youths nationwide between the ages of ten and seventeen has seen or knows someone who has been shot. (Source: *Newsweek*/Children's Defense Fund poll.)
- Children under the age of eighteen are 244 percent more likely to be killed by guns today than they were in 1986. (Source: FBI Uniform Crime Reports.)

Even children who are *not* exposed to direct violence suffer profoundly. Fear of crime and violence in our communities has become as debilitating a social response as any to a world that is presented, realistically or not, as being on the verge of the apocalypse. The resulting helplessness and hopelessness that children feel as prisoners in this state of perpetual hypervigilance is amplified by the fact that they often do not understand what is happening around them and have no idea what to do to escape.

This fear of crime can also be depicted statistically:

- More than half the children and 73 percent of the adults questioned in a recent poll said they were afraid of violent crime against them or a family member. (Source: *Newsweek/*Children's Defense Fund poll.)
- Thirty-five percent of young people believe that it is very likely that "my chances of living to a ripe old age will be cut short because of the threat of my being wiped out from guns." (Source: Harvard School of Public Health/Joyce Foundation study.)
- When asked what was the single most important reason they carried a weapon, 41 percent of the young people polled said "for protection against possible attacks by other people." (Source: Harvard School of Public Health/Joyce Foundation study.)

Children living with violence and distrust, whether actual or virtual, are being denied the consistency, predictability and sense of purpose that they need to grow into independent, productive adults.

From the start, our own paranoia about people who are different from us and about the dangers lurking around us places physical and emotional restrictions on our children. After extended periods of living in virtual war zones, children begin to see life as a series of things happening to them over which they have no control, rather than as a process in which they can orchestrate, or at least influence, their future. A variety of related critical social dysfunctions are becoming more and more familiar to us as we watch our children grow: low levels of motivation as they perceive that they have no impact on the world; reactionary behavior patterns coupled with a resistance to behavior management techniques, because they have not developed an understanding of cause and effect; an inability to see themselves clearly, or to take responsibility for their actions, assigning blame to "other" rather than "self"; dissociation from their feelings and desensitization about human life, resulting in increasing instances of senseless harm to, and even murder of, others, including other children. The flight path of these children, our children, will deliver them into a permanent sense of insecurity and inability to deal with any type of conflict as they grow into adults, unless we take immediate steps to ameliorate the damage.

MEDIA LITERACY

An obvious enigma appears: How can we reassure our children that the world is a safe and inviting place for them to explore when the evidence indicates otherwise? How can we instill in them tolerance and respect for all humankind when all sides seem to be equally engaged in brutally deflecting that respect?

It seems that a careful balance must be struck between acceptance of diversity and preparing children for life in an increasingly violent world. And since mass communication is, and will continue to be, a major point of entry for information about their world, children need to learn to become critical viewers and understand how the media, newspapers and television news programming in particular, both report and create what happens in that world.

One key point is this: Unbiased reporting is a myth. Information, events and discoveries are reported by humans who have applied an interpretation that reflects their own personal values and beliefs. News reporting is the product of some organization, usually a for-profit entity, which is devoted to getting it, interpreting it and disseminating it while being sponsored by another for-profit group which has a stake in making sure it gets the largest market share of viewers.

With fewer adults around to guide children in making their media choices, and then to help them interpret what they see and read, many children have difficulty understanding the difference between reality and the constructed world of the media. Because the profit motive is a critical factor in determining both what and how the news is presented, and conflict and violence are clearly major selling points, children should be taught to ask some essential questions about the print or broadcast news they choose.

Bias

Developing critical viewing skills does not mean distrusting all elements of a news program or news article automatically. It is crucial, however, that children understand how the news makers' perceptions and decisions shape their world. Stereotyping, for example, is particularly dismaying in the mass media. Since reporters have to condense their information into smaller and smaller "sound bites," they don't have the time to profile fully the people about whom they are reporting. Yet they must quickly convey a clear picture of the appearance and motivation of the people in the news. In such situations, it is easy to rely on stereotypes.

Language

During our rescue mission in Somalia a few years ago, a military spokesperson said in reference to why some of their soldiers were caught in an attack, "The organic assets didn't arrive on time," meaning support troops. In press briefings, civilian casualties are referred to as "collateral damage." "Ethnic cleansing" has become the standard news phrase for genocide, and "takeovers" and "kill the competition" are expressions regularly used in reporting about the corporate world. The distinctive feature of this language is that humankind is buried in antiseptic jargon.

On the other hand, random instances of violence or disaster are frequently described in the most gruesome, sensationalized manner, making the event seem more spectacular—seriously distorting our worldview—in the attempt to attract the largest audience share.

Acceleration of News

Two hundred years ago, it took weeks to learn that a peace treaty had been signed, a president had died, or another territory had been added to our country. Today, the press are often the first on the scene, and we are there with them to greet the soldiers through the magic of instantaneous broadcasts. Leaders often communicate to one another through their televised speeches, and decisions are made based not on mediation and negotiation, but on what the content of the CNN broadcast is on a particular day.

The prominent position that we have given the news media in our lives allows our children to read, see and hear much more than they ever have before. They now have instant and repeated access to sounds and images of starving orphans in Somalia, fighting in Bosnia, local scenes of domestic and community violence, and everything in between. Teaching children to be media literate helps them sort out truth from fiction and fact from opinion, giving them a healthy respect for the world without being misled into thinking that everyone they see is a potential danger to their body and soul.

RESPONDING TO KIDS' CONCERNS

On almost any day of the year, there are some corners of our cities, towns and neighborhoods where hatred, conflict and war are being waged. Whether they are active participants or not, our children are never exempt from the blight of these conflicts. In conflict- and violence-ridden areas, everything that creates equilibrium in a child's life is disrupted, including mental and physical health. And studies have shown that if children learn that hatred and conflict are the only options, those behaviors become normalized to them, the negative input becoming ingrained. These children will be more likely to perpetuate that course of action into their adult lives, and to pass it on to subsequent generations.

These children can tell us a great deal about the dynamics of injury and danger. But the impact of what children can tell us depends on what we as adults are prepared to hear. How can we best respond to children's concerns? And what do we do with this information?

Listening

Conflict and violence are on the minds of even our youngest children. We must listen to them as they express these concerns to us, and take them seriously. If we remain silent or ignore their fears, the message we send is that neither they nor their anxieties are important to us.

Reassure them wherever possible. One young child during the Gulf War thought that the Iraqis were going to bomb his school. More recently, another child began having nightmares about a serial killer she saw captured on a television news broadcast. In these cases, simple and straightforward information can be comforting.

Above all, be honest about your own apprehensions. It is far more frightening for children to feel that their care givers are hiding something from them or are too scared to talk than to hear them express their own uneasiness.

Engaging

Today's children feel that they are inheriting a dangerous world. They are angry at us for the increases in racism, hatred, conflict, and violence; for having allowed the decay to happen; for tragically abandoning them to their dire standing as children without a childhood.

But hatred, conflict and violence aren't just things that happen *to* people. They are problems caused *by* people. If, either through our example or our reluctance to address the issues, we allow our children to remain ignorant about one another's differences, we are contributing to the problems. A much more proactive response is to help our children convert these problems into opportunities to meet the challenges of our social ills. We can encourage children to write to their political leaders and newspapers to express their views. They can communicate their feelings through art, poetry, dance or song, and exhibit them to have their feelings acknowledged publicly. As they grow older, they can gather information that helps them understand the issues, inform and educate their peers, and mobilize them to further action. They can participate in humanitarian efforts, advocate on behalf of children and provide inspiration for others to do the same.

A future without violence and hatred is impossible to achieve if our children have been raised to be passive consumers of violence, racial and gender bias and militarism in their toys, books, games and media. Children learn how to be adults from us.

Whether we show by example, or "approve" violence, stereotyping and other forms of brutality by allowing our children to watch certain programs or play with certain toys, we can just as easily lead them down a better, brighter path.

We are all concerned with what our children encounter in today's world, and what its effects might be on subsequent generations. It is time we involve them in helping create the solutions, despite the unknowns and the complexity of our political and social systems. If all of us bring even a fraction of our intellectual, professional and moral resources to bear on the issues of violence and conflict, listen to our children about their concerns and fears, and guide them toward effective action, we might have a shot at securing a better future for them and for ourselves.

STRAIGHT TALK

"TV is the single most significant factor contributing to violence in America."

TED TURNER,
testifying before a congressional subcommittee

DID YOU KNOW?

How to Detect Bias in the News

You can become a more aware news reader or viewer by watching for the following journalistic techniques that allow bias to "creep in" to the news:

- *Bias through selection and omission*
  An editor can express a bias by choosing to use or not to use a specific news item. Within a given story, some

(continued)

details can be ignored, others included, to give readers or viewers a different opinion about the events reported. If, during a speech, a few people boo, for example, the reaction can be described as "remarks greeted by jeers" or it can be ignored as a "handful of dissidents." Bias through omission is difficult to detect. Only by comparing news reports from a wide variety of outlets can the form of bias be observed.

- *Bias through placement*
Readers of papers judge first-page stories to be more significant than those buried in the back. Television and radio newscasts run what they perceive to be the most important stories first and leave the less significant for later. Where a story is placed, therefore, influences what a reader or viewer thinks about its importance.

- *Bias by headline*
Many people read only the headlines of news items. These can summarize as well as present carefully hidden bias and prejudices. They can convey excitement where little exists. They can express approval or condemnation.

- *Bias by photos, captions and camera angles*
Some pictures flatter a person; others make the person look unpleasant. A paper can choose photos to influence opinion about, for example, a candidate for election. On television, the choice of which visual images to display is extremely important. The captions that newspapers run below photos are also a potential source of bias.

- *Bias through use of names and titles*
News media often use labels and titles to describe people, places and events. A person can be called an "ex-

(continued)

con" or be referred to as someone who "served time twenty years ago for a minor offense." Whether a person is described as a "terrorist" or a "freedom fighter" is a clear indication of editorial bias.

- *Bias through statistics and crowd counts*
  To make a disaster seem more spectacular (and therefore worthy of reading), numbers can be inflated. "A hundred injured in air crash" can be the same as "only minor injuries in air crash," reflecting the opinion of the person doing the counting.

- *Bias by source control*
  To detect bias, always consider where the news item comes from. Is the information supplied by a reporter, an eyewitness, police or fire officials, executives, or elected or appointed government officials? Each may have a particular bias that is introduced into the story. Companies and public relations directors supply news outlets with puff pieces through news releases, photos or videos. Often news outlets depend on pseudo-events (demonstrations, sit-ins, ribbon cuttings, speeches and ceremonies) that take place mainly to gain news coverage.

- *Bias by word choice and tone*
  Showing the same kind of bias that appears in headlines, the use of positive or negative words, or words with particular connotations, can strongly influence the reader or viewer.

(Reprinted with permission from *Newskit: A Consumer's Guide to News Media,* The Learning Seed Company, 21250 N. Andover Road, Kilder, IL 60047, 1989.)

HOW DO YOU RATE?

Checklist for Evaluating News Programs

YES NO

☐ ☐ Does the program present minority groups positively, showing them in situations that enhance their image?

☐ ☐ Does the program present gender roles in a positive way? Is the news told from a male or female point of view?

☐ ☐ Is the program free of age stereotypes? Does it portray teenagers predominantly as delinquents, young children as incompetent, older people as flighty?

☐ ☐ Does the program separate fact from fantasy?

☐ ☐ Does it promote nonviolent conflict resolution skills?

☐ ☐ Is it appropriate to your value system?

☐ ☐ Does the program separate advertisements from program content?

☐ ☐ Does the program depict only the "bad" side of the news, or does it include stories about the positive aspects of humankind also?

☐ ☐ Are positive stories given the same importance as negative or violent stories?

FOR YOUR INFORMATION

Center for Media Literacy

The Center for Media Literacy is the nation's largest producer and distributor of media literacy resources to assist people in helping our children to understand, interpret, analyze and evaluate the powerful images, words and sounds that make up our contemporary mass media culture.

Membership privileges include a discount on all of their video and print resources; quarterly issues of *Connect*, featuring background articles on timely media topics, practical tips and techniques and reviews of the latest resources for implementing media literacy; "Media Literacy Basics" pages that provide tools for teaching and learning about TV, films, videos and advertising; and access to their information network and helpline.

For more information, contact

Center for Media Literacy (formerly Center for Media and Values)
1962 S. Shenandoah Street
Los Angeles, CA 90034
310-559-2944 phone
310-559-9396 fax

FOR YOUR INFORMATION

Beyond TV: Activities for Using Video with Children

This book is for people who have been feeling as if they are competing with television for children's attention, and losing. In this volume are hundreds of suggestions for using videos to explore important concepts and skills. Classroom teachers and library media specialists at the elementary school level will especially like this practical guide for turning young "vidiots" into thoughtful, critical viewers.

Beyond TV: Activities for Using Video with Children
Martha Dewing
ABC-CLIO, Inc.
130 Cremona Drive
Santa Barbara, CA 93117
805-968-1911 phone
805-685-9685 fax
1992
ISBN 0-8743-6601-1

EXPRESSING YOUR CONCERNS

Write to these people to praise or criticize their news programming:

ABC-TV
American Broadcasting
  Company
Bob Iger, President and CEO
77 W. 66th Street
New York, NY 10023
212-456-7777 phone
212-456-4866 fax

NBC
National Broadcasting Company
Robert Wright, President and
  CEO
30 Rockefeller Center
New York, NY 10112
212-664-4444 phone
212-664-7234 fax

CNN (Cable News Network)
TBS (Superstation)
TNT (Turner Network
  Television)
Turner Educational Services
1 CNN Center
Atlanta, GA 30348-5366
404-827-1500 phone
404-681-3578 fax

CBS
Columbia Broadcasting Company
Lawrence Tisch, President
51 W. 52nd Street
New York, NY 10019
212-975-4321 phone
212-975-4082 fax

Corporation for Public
  Broadcasting
901 E. St. NW
Washington, DC 20004-2037

ESPN
935 Middle Street
Bristol, CT 06010
203-585-2000 phone
203-585-2213 fax

WHAT YOU CAN DO

In the current social climate, it is not a good idea to ban war play. Children are often attracted to what is forbidden anyway, and there is a danger in making a child feel guilty about having to sneak access to what is popular. But simply remaining mute, creating an "anything goes" atmosphere, does not contribute to a child's healthy development either. Here are some tips to consider when making your choices about these issues with your children:

War Toys

- Know what the influences are on your children. What television programs do they watch? What is the content of the programming? What behavior have they picked up from the programming to use in interactions with their peers?

- Visit the toy store in advance of taking your children there and establish some structure for the childrens' subsequent visit. This is much easier than setting a child free—a child who has been primed to consume through television and other media—awash in a sea of coveted objects.

- Read the descriptions on the packages of toys at the store.

- Help your children to evaluate their toys. If the toy doesn't look exactly like the advertisement, if it doesn't do what it did on television, or if it falls apart because it is cheaply made, use these occasions as a basis to discuss what they have learned from the experiences.

- Understand all the dangers inherent in playing with toy guns and stop giving them to your children. They may still use a stick or other object as a gun, but buying toy guns tells them that you think guns are okay and should be used as a way to solve conflicts.

- Buy as few single-purpose war toys as possible, choosing the most open-ended designs whose functions are not fully defined by their appearance, the images on the package, or the television program that advertises it.

- Monitor the amount of time your children are involved in war play. They might need some help extricating themselves from that into other compelling types of play.

- Help your children learn to use playthings in new ways. Try making suggestions that help your children see that there are more possibilities for a toy than those dictated by the manufacturer.

- Encourage your children to make their own toys and props. Deciding what to make, how to construct them and then actually producing them offers opportunities for complex, critical thinking, problem solving and a feeling of accomplishment. When children make their own toys, they reclaim ownership of their play as their ideas become part of the process.

- Go public with your protests. Public opinion forced G.I. Joe off the shelves during the Vietnam War, and more recently convinced a Massachusetts-based toy retailer to burn its fake weapons. Political and community action works. Arrange a meeting with the manager of your local toy store and ask him or her not to carry war toys. Hold a public hearing on war toys and cartoons. Write letters of protest to local television stations that air violent cartoons. Put on an alternative toy fair.
- Change the rules of war games to make them cooperative.
- As a family, learn to play nonviolent games that require cooperation among players.
- Make your home a "violence free" zone and ask others not to bring war toys into your home.
- Collect war toys from willing children in your neighborhood and give them a public burial with an appropriate eulogy.
- Inform your childrens' teachers about your disapproval of the presence of war toys and your support of a weapons- and violence-free zone at the school. Spearhead a fund-raising drive to stock the zone with nonviolent and cooperative games and toys.
- Talk to your children about their fears and anxieties rather than simply arm them with toy weapons.

Video Games

- Publishers and media production companies take years to develop most learning materials. Schools take their time, also, to evaluate and adopt new texts. Many parents and teachers, however, race to get the latest games for their children with only a cursory knowledge of their contents. Take your time in choosing what video games your children play.

- Play the games yourself. If you take an active role in previewing them, you will get to know the games and build the knowledge base to argue intelligently with your child about your decisions.

- Don't ban video games if your child is already playing them on a regular basis. Find the moral in the madness instead. Discuss with them the content of any game that your children want to play. Besides bringing up the obvious excess of violence, point out the more subtle messages the game is communicating, such as racism, sexism and other types of discrimination.

- Purchase or rent nonviolent games that require two or more players, and encourage your child to invite others over to play.

EXPRESSING YOUR CONCERNS

Write to these people if you have questions and concerns about your children's video games and toys:

Nintendo of America Inc.
Minoru Aratawa, President
4820 150th Avenue NE
Redmond, WA 98052-5111
206-882-2040 phone
206-882-3585 fax

SEGA of America
Tom Kalinski, President
P.O. Box 8097
Redwood City, CA 94063
415-591-7529 phone

HOW DO YOU RATE?

Checklist for Choosing Good Toys

YES NO

☐ ☐ Is the toy safe?

☐ ☐ Does it stimulate creativity?

☐ ☐ Is it free of stereotypes?

☐ ☐ Does it encourage sharing or cooperation?

☐ ☐ Does it nurture nonviolent conflict resolution skills?

☐ ☐ Is it appropriate to your value system?

☐ ☐ Is it worth the price?

☐ ☐ Is the packaging truthful and not excessive?

☐ ☐ Does it help develop or strengthen skills?

☐ ☐ Does it teach children to use their power and skills in a positive way?

(Source: War Resisters League.)

ACCLAIM
Allyne Mills, Director of Public
  Relations
71 Audrey Avenue
Oyster Bay, NY 11771
516-624-8888 phone
516-624-2181 fax

Toys 'R' Us Corporation
Robert Nakasone, President
461 From Road
Paramus, NJ 07652
201-262-7800 phone
201-262-8919 fax

Television

- Guide what your children watch on television and limit their viewing time. Although this is an old recommendation, it is more easily accomplished now with the help of a recent invention: an electronic lock that permits parents to preset which programs, channels and times they want to make available to their children.
- Plan your children's viewing times with them. Giving them choices within certain guidelines, use a TV guide or newspaper listing to help the children decide in advance which shows to see for the week. And then turn the television off when those shows are over.
- Watch television with your children. If you don't know about the material to which they are exposed, you will be ill-equipped to make decisions about which programs should be off-limits to them.
- Offer alternatives to watching television. Use a VCR and good children's movies, or substitute open-ended activities that offer opportunities to be active and creative.
- Teach your children to be "stereotype detectives": Have them find television characters who depict racial, ethnic, gender, and other stereotypes and talk to them about how those characters might have been portrayed better.
- Your consumer dollar can be a strong force against bad programming. Boycott products produced by sponsors of objectionable programs, and let the company, your local station and your local newspaper know that you are doing it and why.
- It took twenty-five years to get the Children's Television Act (which requires television stations to provide educational viewing choices for children) written into law, but it

won't be enforced unless we hold television stations accountable. Lobbying works best on the local level. "A station doesn't want to look like Godzilla in its own community," says Peggy Charren, founder of Action for Children's Television. Remind your local stations that failure to provide educational programming could result in the stations losing their licenses. If you are uncertain about the stations' plans and activities in this regard, ask to see the public file that the law requires them to maintain containing the information.

- Conversely, express your thanks to networks, sponsors and local stations, both privately and publicly, for showing programs that support your values and viewpoints.

- Work with your local stations to produce and offer programs and services designed to support children and families: quality children's shows from around the world, programs produced by children themselves and programs designed to support parents in their efforts to raise healthy and happy children.

- If you are a doctor, dentist or other medical professional whose office has a waiting room, post a sign stating that your office is a "television-free zone," and provide other options for keeping your patients and clients engaged while they wait.

- Record objectionable programs on your VCR and send them to the Federal Communications Commission with a letter identifying the city and state from which the broadcast aired, the call letters of the station and the reasons you object to it. Address your tapes and letters to: Complaints and Investigative Branch, Enforcement Division, Federal Communications Commission, 2025 M Street, N.W., Washington, DC 20554.

EXPRESSING YOUR CONCERNS

Write to these people if you have questions and concerns about commercial television programming:

ABC-TV
American Broadcasting
  Company
Bob Iger, President and CEO
77 W. 66th Street
New York, NY 10023
212-456-7777 phone
212-456-4866 fax

NBC
National Broadcasting Company
Robert Wright, President and
  CEO
30 Rockefeller Center
New York, NY 10112
212-664-4444 phone
212-664-7234 fax

Fox Broadcasting Company
40 W. 57th St.
New York, NY 10019

CBS
Columbia Broadcasting
  Company
Lawrence Tisch, President
51 W. 52nd Street
New York, NY 10019
212-975-4321 phone
212-975-4082 fax

CNN (Cable News Network)
TBS (Superstation)
TNT (Turner Network
  Television)
Turner Educational Services
1 CNN Center
Atlanta, GA 30348-5366
404-827-1500 phone
404-681-3578 fax

Media Literacy

- The National Telemedia Council states that it's not what you watch on television, but how you watch it. Help your children analyze all of the programs they watch. Discuss with them how images and content form impressions.

- Have your children compare newspaper stories and news broadcasts about actual acts of violence with television dramas about violence. Ask them to tell you how they think real life acts of violence differ from those depicted on television.

- Give your children journals and ask them to jot down a note about every reference to aggression in the media that they encounter during a week's time, real or fictitious. Have them include not only television and newspaper accounts, but images and stories from magazines, billboards, music, advertisements for toys, posters, and so on. Not only will this give you a platform from which to begin a serious dialogue about aggression and violence, but you will also have a clearer concept of the sheer quantity of aggressive messages to which your children are exposed on a daily basis.

- Hang a world map somewhere in your home. This will give your children a sense of distance from zones of war and conflict, while enabling you to talk about different parts of the world as you point them out.

- Have your children cut out news stories about several ethnic, racial or other minority groups for one month. Give them folders to keep their stories separate according to group. At the end of the month, review the contents of the folders with them. Are the images of blacks in the news mostly negative? How many references are there to Hispan-

HOW DO YOU RATE?

Checklist for Choosing Nonviolent Television Shows

YES NO

☐ ☐ Does violence drive the story line? Would there even be a story without the violence?

☐ ☐ Is the hero ever safe in this show?

☐ ☐ Would it be difficult to sum up the story in this program without making at least one reference to an act of violence?

☐ ☐ When people die on this program, do they simply disappear?

☐ ☐ Is anyone ever shown mourning when a person is killed or seriously injured?

☐ ☐ Do the protagonists in the story have any bad qualities?

☐ ☐ Do the "good guys" win?

☐ ☐ Do the "bad guys" have family or friends who will care if they get hurt or killed?

ics? Native Americans? Asians? Are the positive articles on Asians about academic success? Are the positive articles about blacks about athletics? Take this opportunity to talk to your children about negative effects of stereotyping, using news bias as an example.

Responding to Your Children

- Translate large and confusing events into smaller concrete terms for your younger children, and give only as much detail as the child asks for. Lengthy explanations of political or economic forces won't help your child understand conflict and violence, but short answers in age-appropriate language will.

- Ask your child's teacher for help by encouraging the children to talk about events in the news that might be scary. Children feel better when they hear that the reactions of their peers mirror their own, and the group discussion about an event might lead to some concrete action on the part of the children.

- When listening to your children, consider the following tips:

  1. Do not let other noise or activity distract you. Pay attention to the verbal *and* nonverbal cues your children are expressing.
  2. Look for the important theme that the children are communicating to you. It may be hidden with other issues.
  3. Wait before you respond, making sure the children have expressed what they need to say about their feelings.
  4. Paraphrase what you heard from the child, and ask if that's what she was saying to you.
  5. Share your feelings and concerns with children in age-appropriate terms. Take time to explain. And affirm them for having talked to you.

CHAPTER TWO

Evaluating Your Child's Literature

Children's literature, sometimes seen as lighthearted, a simple world of make-believe, is a powerful force for helping children understand their homes and communities. Before they can toddle, children hear familiar stories repeated again and again, often from the secure vantage point of a mother's, father's or other trusted care giver's lap. The messages they learn are forever associated with the security of those arms.

Children's books can greatly expand a child's imagination. Moral and ethical beliefs can be conveyed through stories. Children can develop a strong self-image through reading. And in a world where television monopolizes our lives, children's literature is a wonderful way to establish or repair the relationship between children and adults.

Books and other printed materials can also provide a channel through which children can learn to respect the diverse groups of people in the world around them. Children can learn that beneath the surface differences of color or country of origin, all people have feelings of love, sadness, fear, justice and tenderness.

Unfortunately, many children's books reflect a variety of biases. Sexism and racism are among the most prevalent offenders. Simply by choosing such literature—often with the most innocent of intentions—parents, teachers and those who work with children can reinforce and perpetuate a wide range of common societal stereotypes. It is especially harmful to support stereotypical portrayals in the first decade of a child's life, when clear concepts of self and others are just being formed. It only becomes more difficult later in their lives for them to respect and appreciate differences. Because books are a significant part of a young child's life, both at home and in child care settings, those who work with children should be scrupulous in their selection of books and resource materials that are free of bias and stereotypes.

WHAT DOES IT MEAN?

Sexism

Attitudes and actions that define a person's role in life according to gender, relegating that person to secondary and inferior status in society; any attitude, action or institutional practice that subordinates people because of their gender.

Racism

The belief that assigns to people an inferior or limited role based on race or skin color, with the assumption that the racial characteristics determine a person's capacities and behavior. This includes the imposition of one ethnic group's culture in such a way as to withhold respect for, to demean or to destroy the cultures of other races. The glorification of one race over others and the consistent exclusion of certain races are also instances of racism.

People of color

All the different national or ethnic groups that are targets of racism. Use of this inclusive term is not intended to deny the significant cultural and historic differences among these groups.

Bias

Any attitude, belief or feeling that results in and helps to justify unfair treatment of an individual because of his or her identity.

Prejudice

An attitude, opinion or feeling formed without adequate prior knowledge, thought or reason. Prejudice can be prejudgment for or against any person, group or gender.

Stereotype

An oversimplified generalization about people from any group—such as ethnic, racial, religious—which usually carries derogatory implications.

SEXISM

Girls growing up now are told that they can be anything they want to be. They can do anything, feel anything, say anything. One can wonder why, then, girls and women are portrayed in children's literature as being more passive than active, more nurturing than adventuresome, sweet and weak rather than bold and strong.

Consider, for example, what traditional fairy tales say about women. The prevailing attributes awarded to female characters in most fairy tales are incompetence and helplessness, extreme physical appearance and secondary citizenship, all couched in strict adherence to traditional roles.

Heroines cannot take care of themselves. In most of "Hansel and Gretel," for example, Gretel is frightened and tearful in the face of adversity while her brother, Hansel, is strong, intelligent and brave. Cinderella is helped by a woman, her fairy godmother, but in the end is rescued from her poverty and unhappy home by a prince. Snow White is saved from death by a hunter, assisted by male dwarfs, then finally rescued by a handsome prince. Red Riding Hood, too, is saved from death by a hunter, whereupon she vows never again to wander. Apparently being adventurous is too dangerous for girls.

STRAIGHT TALK

"Psychological oppression in the form of sex role clearly conveys to girls from the earliest ages that their nature is to be submissive, servile and repressed . . . In addition, both men and women have come to realize the effects on men of . . . sex role stereotyping, the crippling pressure to compete, to achieve, to produce, to stifle emotion, sensitivity and gentleness, all taking their toll in psychic and physical traumas."

The Association of Women Psychologists

HOW DO YOU RATE?

Checklist for Sexism in Children's Literature

YES   NO

☐ ☐   Are girls rewarded for skills and competence rather than beauty?

☐ ☐   Is a realistic proportion of mothers shown at work outside the home?

☐ ☐   Are some of their jobs other than administrative or technical jobs?

☐ ☐   Are fathers shown raising or spending time with children?

☐ ☐   Do all members of the family participate equally in household chores?

☐ ☐   Do girls and boys participate equally in physical activities?

☐ ☐   Do girls and boys participate equally in intellectual activities?

☐ ☐   Do male and female characters respect each other as equals?

☐ ☐   Are both girls and boys shown to be self-reliant, clever and brave—capable of facing their own problems and finding their own solutions?

(continued)

YES NO

☐ ☐ Are there any derogatory sex-stereotyped characterizations, such as "Boys make the best architects," or "Girls are silly"?

☐ ☐ Are both girls and boys shown as having a wide range of sensibilities, feelings and responses?

☐ ☐ Is the male pronoun (e.g., mankind, he) used to refer to all people?

☐ ☐ Are girls' accomplishments, not their clothing or features, emphasized?

☐ ☐ Are nonhuman characters and their relationships personified in sex stereotypes (e.g., dogs depicted as masculine, cats as feminine)?

☐ ☐ Are the women and girls portrayed as docile and passive and in need of help?

☐ ☐ Does the material reflect the conditions and contributions of women in today's society?

☐ ☐ Are women in cultures other than the dominant one depicted accurately?

☐ ☐ Are traits such as strength, compassion, initiative, warmth and courage treated as human rather than gender-specific?

☐ ☐ Does the material encourage both girls and boys to see themselves as human beings with an equal right to all benefits and choices?

Many fairy tales feature beautiful women whose fulfillment is derived from handsome men and from marriage. Their beauty, and not their personality or actions, defines them and makes them valuable to others. In some, the women are featured as shrews, ugly witches or vain and wicked stepmothers. These female characters are most often introduced as inferior people or as possessions of men. "Hansel and Gretel" begins: "Close to a large forest lived a woodcutter, with his wife and two children." "Rumpelstiltskin" begins: "There once was a miller who was very poor, but he had a beautiful daughter." "Cinderella" begins: "There once was an honest gentleman who took for his second wife the proudest and most disagreeable lady in the whole country."

All the while these beautiful women are engaged in traditional roles, those of wife, mother and housewife, with abject satisfaction. Typical is the passage in "Snow White" where the dwarfs ask her to live with them: " 'You could sew and mend, and keep everything tidy.' This made Snow White very happy. 'Oh, thank you,' she said. 'I could want nothing better.' "

Unlike the female characters, males in fairy tales are most often portrayed as courageous, adventurous, powerful, intelligent and enterprising. "Puss in Boots" is creative and industrious. Jack, of beanstalk fame, is daring and resourceful in defeating the giant and saving his mother and himself from poverty. Hansel is brave, inventive and intelligent, as well as being an emotional bulwark for Gretel to lean on.

Even men who do negative things are often absolved—if not rewarded—for their negative behavior. Hansel and Gretel's father suffers only temporarily for his deeds and is rewarded by getting his children back—plus a small fortune. The soldier in "The Tinder Box" kills a witch after she provides him with great wealth, kills a king and a queen in order to have their daughter, and ends up a king himself as a reward for his avarice. When the poor father in "Rumpelstiltskin" lies to the king about his daughter's ability to spin straw into gold, he gets her into all kinds of trouble but is never admonished for his actions. This pattern, a form of literary distributive justice, occurs again and again throughout the fairy tale canon.

The uniformity of this type of gender stereotyping is far from limited to fairy tales. Studies on current children's literature have shown that boys have been written about more than girls; that there has been an imbalance in the frequency with which males and females occupy leading roles; and that males and females, both as children and adults, have most often been depicted in traditional roles. Even more recent classics and award-winning books are not free of sex bias.

In *Little Women*, Mother March gives this advice to Jo: " 'To be loved and chosen by a good man is the best and sweetest thing which can happen to a woman. Prepare for it, so when the happy day comes, you may feel ready for the duties and worthy of the joy.' " More recently, the duality is described in this example for younger children, the 1970 book *Glad to Be a Boy, Glad to Be a Girl*, still on the shelves in many libraries:

Boys are doctors; girls are nurses.
Boys are football players; girls are cheerleaders.
Boys invent things; girls use things boys invent.
Boys fix things; girls need things fixed.
Boys are Presidents; girls are First Ladies.

Turning the tables, can't boys do anything and be anything and feel anything, too? Why is it then that boys aren't allowed to cry? Why is becoming a ballet dancer, a children's librarian or an artist seen as less desirable for boys than becoming a basketball player, a business executive or President of the United States? Why do men have to be pictured as reading the paper, fixing the plumbing or disciplining their children? Boys need emancipation, too.

These stereotypical views ultimately create diminished expectations of both girls *and* boys, limiting their options even before they begin to explore them. Breaking out of the trap wherein gender determines what is and isn't possible requires a keen eye and some incisive questioning when reviewing what your children are reading.

DID YOU KNOW?

Frequently Depicted Stereotypes in Children's Literature

Male	Female
active	passive
brave	frightened
strong	weak
intelligent, logical	unintelligent, illogical
quiet, easygoing	shrewish, nagging
messy	neat
tall	short
mechanical	inept
independent	dependent
leader, innovator	follower, conformer
as parent, plays with kids	as parent, nurtures kids

(continued)

Asian Male	Asian Female
smiling, polite, small	sweet, well-behaved girl
servile, bowing	sexy, sweet "China Doll"
buck-toothed and squinty-eyed	evil "Dragon Lady"
mystical, inscrutable and wise	overbearing, old-fashioned
sinister and sly	
super student	

African American Male	African American Female
shuffling, eye-rolling comic	big-bosomed "mammy," loyal to whites
gentle, self-sacrificing older man	big, bossy mother or maid
athletic super-jock	sexy temptress
smooth-talking con-man ..	stupid, but sweet, little girl
super-stud	tragic mulatto
exotic primitive	

Latino	Latina
sombrero-wearing, serape-clad	hardworking, poor, submissive
taking siesta near cactus or burro	religious mother of many
ignorant, cheerful, lazy	sweet, small, shy, gentle

(continued)

Latino (cont.)	Latina (cont.)
sneaky, knife-wielding bandit	sexy, loud, fiery
teenage gang member	undereducated, submissive
impoverished migrant worker	
unemployed barrio dweller	

Native American Male	Native American Female
savage, bloodthirsty "native"	heavyset, workhorse "squaw"
stoic, loyal follower	Indian princess
drunken comic or mean thief	
wise old chief	
evil medicine man	

(Source: *Guidelines for Selecting Bias-Free Textbooks and Storybooks*, 1980, Council on Interracial Books for Children.)

RACISM

The race inequality in much of children's literature is even more alarming than gender stereotyping. No more than twenty-five years ago, children's literature treated minorities either stereotypically and as objects of ridicule, or ignored them completely.

The civil rights movement helped bring about a change in the ways minorities were depicted. But the numbers were still unbalanced. By the 1980s, only about 1 percent of children's books being published yearly were about African Americans, though African Americans represent an increasingly larger portion of our total population, and the picture continues to be depressing for other minority groups, too. While the children's literature genre no longer presents an all-white world to the same extent as it once did, only about 10 percent of the almost five thousand children's books published each year in the United States are multicultural in nature. Of those, fewer than fifty titles annually have been written by and about Native American and Asian peoples.

> **STRAIGHT TALK**
>
> "If black children or Native Americans or Asians don't see themselves in books, they won't see themselves as important people. And we will be sending that message to white children, too."
>
> ROBERTA LONG,
> *professor of children's literature*

Until recently, most of the children's books featuring Native American themes perpetuated negative stereotypes, with Indians portrayed as uncivilized, simple, inarticulate and either hateful, bloodthirsty savages or dependent on those who came to colonize their territories. The newest stereotype of Native Americans, developed after they were placed on reservations decades ago, depicts them as defrauded, dispossessed victims, alcoholics unable to cope or assimilate.

Some people will argue that the tender years of childhood are not the right time to be worrying about these potentially divisive issues, and that talking about variety in people only reinforces their differences and not their unifying common needs. But children are aware of gender and race differences by the age of two. By age four, they have already formed attitudes about race. Children's literature can provide all children with pathways to knowledge about themselves and classmates about whom they know very little. By exposing children early on to multicultural literature, not only can prejudice be reduced, but it can help to prevent it entirely.

HOW DO YOU RATE?

Checklist for Racism in Children's Literature

YES NO

☐ ☐ Are illustrations true to the people depicted, or are they caricatures or stereotypes?

☐ ☐ Do illustrations of regional minorities present accurate representations of living conditions, dress styles, and so on?

☐ ☐ Are people of color shown in a variety of lifestyles?

(continued)

YES NO

☐ ☐   Does the material emphasize that every group has its achievers, thinkers, writers, artists, scientists, builders and political leaders?

☐ ☐   Do the materials describe the achievements of all people in a similar fashion?

☐ ☐   Does the story focus on problems and issues that provide insight into the experience of racial and ethnic groups?

☐ ☐   Does the story focus on interactions between racial or minority groups and the dominant culture?

☐ ☐   Does it portray the minority culture as "problem oriented"?

☐ ☐   Is prejudice treated as a given without explanation?

☐ ☐   Are people of color depicted with the same socioeconomic range as whites?

☐ ☐   Are people of color shown engaged in problem-solving activities in all professional areas in business, community and world affairs?

☐ ☐   Are people of color central characters in the story?

☐ ☐   Are dialects considered integral to the story as part of our rich cultural heritage?

(continued)

YES	NO	
☐	☐	Does the narrative convey a theme that is realistic, believable and not patronizing?
☐	☐	Is bilingualism considered an asset to the characters?
☐	☐	Are both female and male members of minority groups depicted in situations which exhibit them as worthy models to emulate?
☐	☐	Does the material help children to recognize both the basic similarities among all people as well as the uniqueness of the individual?
☐	☐	Do minority faces show individuality and not all look alike?
☐	☐	Do whites in the story have power and make decisions while nonwhites function in subservient roles?
☐	☐	Are achievements of minority women and girls shown?

At a time when the positive connotations of "white" and the negative connotations of "black" are being revised internationally, when racial and ethnic tensions are flaring across the country and when Americans are handicapped by their lack of understanding about others who are different from them, it seems imperative to stop using stories in which all of the beautiful and good women are fair and white, the history and achievements of people of color are missing and the background, setting and central themes are not racially diverse. Showing racial, ethnic and gender balance in depictions of schools, crowds, stores, and social gatherings, and at all levels of employment, is simply a mirror of today's pluralistic society. Our children are forming their race and gender ideas right now. Now is the time to introduce them to literature that opens the doors to full human potential for every child.

WHAT YOU CAN DO

- Research the books in your school and public libraries. If books are to be used to help young people understand the value of living in a multicultural world, stories should be available in which people of all kinds are portrayed as protagonists and problem solvers, capable of interacting and collaborating in integrated settings.
- Always read every book before sharing it with your children, familiarizing yourself with the story and its characters. Choose books that contain a balance of gender and racial characters. When you read, label neutral characters as *both* female and male to balance representation.
- Involve the children as you read to them. Ask them questions about the story as you read.
- Talk about your own childhood heroes and why you admired them. Use this conversation as a springboard to let your children tell you what they like best about their heroes. If their heroes are fictional, help them think about real people who have some of the same characteristics.
- Many textbook manufacturers are responding to the changes in our society by requiring that textbook illustrations include equal and accurate representations of women and minorities. Children's book publishers, however,

haven't developed a parallel standard. Write to publishers alerting them to the fact that their continually presenting an unbalanced ratio of characters, whether the imbalance is gender, ethnic, racial or otherwise stereotypical in nature, causes all children to lose out, and ask them to respond by being more inclusive in their publishing choices.

- Many small presses are taking the lead in producing quality multicultural children's literature representing greater population diversity. Support them in their efforts by buying their products which, in turn, will encourage them to produce more multicultural books for the children's literature market.

- Create a demand for multicultural books through group, school and library purchases, sending a powerful message to publishers that multicultural literature is read and enjoyed by all children, not just by the segment of the market about whom the books are written.

- Talk to your local bookseller about promoting the sale of multicultural children's books by holding bilingual readings, emphasizing their commitment to multicultural literature in their newsletters and bringing in multicultural children's authors to speak in their stores.

DID YOU KNOW?

While Caldecott and Newbery award winners may indicate the highest standard in children's literature, they are not necessarily the books teachers actually choose for their classrooms. Studies have shown that:

(continued)

- Elementary teachers who were asked to list their favorite books to read aloud to children reported more books about males than about females; only 21 percent of the books listed contained a female protagonist. (Source: Smith, N.J., Green, M.J., and Scott, C.J. "Making the Literate Environment Equitable," *The Reading Teacher*, No. 40 (1987), 400–407.)

- When *student* teachers were asked to select a book from which they thought children would benefit, 74 percent of the selections featured males as primary characters, while only 19 percent featured females. (Source: Luke, A., Cooke, J., and Luke, C. "The Selective Tradition in Action: Gender Bias in Student Teachers' Selections of Children's Literature," *English Education*, No. 18 (1986), 209–218.)

DID YOU KNOW?

Young children may be even more likely to interpret generic pronouns as referring specifically to one gender, since children react literally to language.

- This level of understanding is demonstrated by children's actual interpretation of masculine pronouns. Evidence suggests that an overwhelming percentage of kindergarten and first grade children (i.e., 96 percent)

(continued)

interpret the word "he" in stories as referring to a boy. (Source: Fisk, W. R. "Responses to 'Neutral' Pronoun Presentations and the Development of Sex Biased Responding," *Developmental Psychology*, No. 21 (1985), 481–485.)

- In a study of 310 school-aged children, only 28 percent of first graders, 32 percent of third graders and 42 percent of fifth graders stated that "he" could refer to both males and females. (Source: Hyde, J. S. "Children's Understanding of Sexist Language," *Developmental Psychology*, No. 20 (1984), 697–706.)

DID YOU KNOW?

Biased Language	Non-Biased Language
mankind, man, men	humankind, people, humanity
the rise of man	the rise of civilization
great men in history	great figures in history
man's achievements	human achievements
Cro-Magnon man	Cro-Magnon people
man and wife	husband and wife; wife and husband
fireman	firefighter
Congressman	member of Congress

(continued)

one-man show	solo performance; individual exhibit
spokesman	representative; spokesperson
chairman	chair; chairperson; moderator
manpower	human energy
brotherhood	community
man-made	manufactured; simulated; hand-built; handmade; machine-made
meter maid	meter reader
housewife	homemaker
forefathers	founders of our country
blackball	prevent; exclude
blackmail	extort; shake down
Jew him down	bargain with him

EXPRESSING YOUR CONCERNS

Publishers have a window of opportunity—and an obligation—to counteract centuries of literary abuse of minorities by breaking them out of their stereotypical confines. By widening their diversity net to include people other than the recognizable standbys or the current media darlings, publishers can create the impression that people of color are a common, not exceptional, part of everyday life. If you feel strongly about supporting this notion, or have other concerns, here is a partial list of national publishers who are major players in the children's book market:

Bantam Doubleday Dell
  Publishing Group, Inc.
1540 Broadway
New York, NY 10036
212-765-6500 or 800-223-6834
  phone
212-782-9575 fax

Dial Books for Young Readers
375 Hudson Street
New York, NY 10014
800-526-0275 phone
212-782-9575 fax

Harcourt Brace Jovanovich
HBJ Children's Book Division
1250 Sixth Avenue
San Diego, CA 92101
619-699-6598

Henry Holt & Co.
115 W. 18th Street
New York, NY 10011
800-488-5233 phone
(801) 977-9712 fax

The Putnam & Grosset Group
200 Madison Avenue
New York, NY 10016
212-951-8700

Random House, Inc.
201 E. 50th Street
New York, NY 10022
212-751-2600

Simon & Schuster
1230 Avenue of the Americas
New York, NY 10020
212-698-7000

William Morrow & Company
1350 Avenue of the Americas
New York, NY 10019
212-261-6500 or 800-843-9389

FOR YOUR INFORMATION

Multicultural Dictionaries

Here are three dictionaries that highlight a diversity of cultures:
The Calypso Alphabet ($13.95) presents twenty-six words from
the varied dialects of the Caribbean islands. Colorful artwork

brings each word to life, and a useful glossary supplements the text.
From:

Henry Holt & Co.
115 W. 18th Street
New York, NY 10011
800-488-5233 phone
(801) 977-9712 fax

The Handmade Alphabet ($14) explores the visual world of signing. The manual, more than a practical tool for teaching youngsters signing, is also a brilliant work of art that captures the beauty of sign language.
From:

Dial Books for Young Readers
375 Hudson Street
New York, NY 10014
800-526-0275 phone
212-782-9575 fax

Alef-Bet: A Hebrew Alphabet Book ($15) introduces young children to modern Hebrew through a very special five-year-old named Gabi. While learning Hebrew, young readers follow Gabi as she dances and plays.
From:

William Morrow & Company
1350 Avenue of the Americas
New York, NY 10019
800-843-9389 or
212-261-6500

HOW DO YOU RATE?

Checklist for the Human Family in Children's Literature

YES NO

☐ ☐ Are single-parent families, families with working mothers, and extended families shown in approximate proportion to their actual occurrence in the population?

☐ ☐ Do single people with satisfying lives and work, including mothers or fathers who may have been divorced or widowed, appear in the stories?

☐ ☐ Is our true pluralistic society depicted, rather than a mythical, typical society?

☐ ☐ Are all lifestyles considered equally valid?

☐ ☐ Are the elderly included in realistic and unpatronizing ways?

☐ ☐ Do the materials perpetuate stereotypical images of the physically or mentally disabled, including helplessness and dependency?

☐ ☐ Is the history of the oppressed equivalent to the presentation of the dominant group?

PART TWO

Home to School

CHAPTER THREE

The School Climate: Creating a Supportive Setting

Historically, America is a country of immigrants. What many of us fail to recognize, however, is that it continues to be so. In fact, we are becoming so diverse a population that the statistical meaning of the word "minority" is losing its significance. Consider the following:

- Between 1980 and 1990, the white population grew by only 7.7 percent nationally. The African American and Hispanic populations grew by 15.8 percent and 34.5 percent respectively.
- The fastest growing group during that decade was Asians, who make up about half of all new immigrants.
- Census projections indicate that by the middle of the twenty-first century, white Americans will become the nation's numerical minority.
- The population is intermarrying with increasing frequency. By the middle of the twenty-first century, the "average" American citizen will trace his or her origins to Africa, Asia,

the Hispanic countries, the Pacific Islands—anywhere but
white Europe.

- The rapid shift in demographics is already evident among
  our youth population. The number of linguistically different
  children is quickly rising and our twenty-five largest city
  school systems have minority student majorities.

- More than 150 languages are represented in schools nationwide, and figures nearing this number occur in some large
  districts.

- Children of color currently make up 30 percent of America's
  youth under age eighteen, and the percentage is increasing.

These demographic changes are real, immutable and accelerat-
ing. The continuing influx of immigrants has reverberated through
every social institution in America, including our schools.

Making the equation more complex, ethnic identification is
not the only criterion that is commonly used to denote differences in culture. Religion, gender, lifestyle, socioeconomic status
all can, and should, be consid-
ered as having distinct cultural
indicators.

STRAIGHT TALK

"We need an essentially new way
of thinking if mankind is to
survive."

ALBERT EINSTEIN,
1946

In a country where one out
of five children lives below
the poverty line, where huge
numbers have been raised in
non-English-speaking homes,
where the characteristic of
"otherness" can be applied to
more children than not in any given classroom, it is imperative
that we understand the depth and breadth of culture—and are
aware of its implications as it drives changes in our schools.

WHO FAILS AND WHO SUCCEEDS?

Contemporary laws, combined with our social norms and sense of justice, theoretically protect the educational rights of all children through equal access to education. These concepts and laws can allow diversity among students to be honored, their knowledge differences appreciated. Why, then, is the drop-out rate for Hispanic students hovering at 45 percent, fully twenty percentage points above the already high national high school drop-out rate of 25 percent? Why are there startling disparities by gender, race and national origin in disciplinary referrals and suspensions in public schools? Why have minority students been suspended from school more often for less serious offenses than their white peers? Why are poor children more likely to fail than children from economically advantaged homes? Why are these "at risk" students more involved in unsafe activities either as victims or aggressors than their majority peers?

One real answer is that American schools in general continue

> **STRAIGHT TALK**
>
> "The President said he was sickened by the random violence among young people and particularly disgusted by an incident in Chicago in which a five-year-old boy was pushed to his death by two ten-year-olds because he refused to steal candy for them. The President wondered aloud how young children could become so cold hearted and then he answered his own question, 'They learn such horrific behavior from adults.' "
>
> CAL THOMAS,
> *"In Search of Values,"*
> Courier Journal,
> *Louisville, Kentucky,*
> *October 23, 1994*

to both perpetuate and communicate the values, power relation-ships and behavioral standards of those for whom schools in this country were originally intended: middle-class Europeans. As a result, students whose cultures are different from that of the school often feel alienated from and rejected by their school system.

Our schools, whether by law or by moral commitment, are responsible for the growth and development of all of our nation's children. To accomplish this, our schools must create environ-ments that are caring, safe and secure for *all* children. The re-luctance or inability of schools to do so is at the heart of their failure to educate the racially, culturally and otherwise "different" children of this country.

WHY KEEP KIDS IN SCHOOL?

In addition to the legal and ethical imperatives for educating all of our children, two seemingly disparate phenomena make it even more critical to do so now: the increase in youth violence and the changing labor market.

Violence

Every day, quarrels among children that used to result in ex-changes of insults, fistfights and bloody noses now end in gun-shots. Every day almost 135,000 students carry guns to school. Every day nearly 200,000 children miss school because of fear of attack by other students, and some 2,000 young people are attacked in school. Every two days, 25 children—an entire class-room—are killed by guns.

The reasons for this raging brutality are clear. Neglected, re-

DID YOU KNOW?

- Every two hours, a child dies from gunshot wounds.
- Guns are the number one cause of death among ten- to twenty-four-year-old black males, and the number two cause of death among all ten- to fourteen-year-olds. While it is true that people, rather than guns, kill teenagers, more than 97 percent of the time the crime is committed with a gun.
- Youth violence and delinquency are costly. The average hospitalization cost for a child injured by a gun is $14,434—enough to pay for a year of college. The Department of Justice reported that holding youth in custody cost U.S. taxpayers $1.7 billion in 1988, at an average annual per resident cost of $29,600, more expensive than paying tuition, room and board at Harvard, Yale or Princeton.
- Every day 1.2 million latchkey children come home to houses in which there are guns. According to a 1993 report by the Secretary's Advisory Committee for Injury Prevention and Control, the impulsiveness to commit a violent act may be aided by ready access to a weapon.
- Almost all teens who kill with guns get them illegally. A twenty-state survey of eleven thousand adolescents found that 41 percent of the boys could obtain a handgun if they wanted to, and two out of three of them say they could get one in twenty-four hours.
- Violence is not just a minority problem. All communities are affected. The firearm homicide death rate for all races and both sexes doubled from 1985 to 1991 for ten- to fourteen-year-olds, and tripled for fifteen- to nineteen-year-olds.

jected cast-off kids turn into bitter, gun-toting criminals more often than not. Weaned on violent video games, toys and media programming, they are desensitized to violence as never before. The presence of violence at school breeds more violence. The fear of attack escalates, more weapons are brought to school, and getting to the next class becomes a matter of survival. The unthinkable has become normal behavior for many children, and they see no functional alternatives.

This fear of violence—and its resulting metal detectors, security guards, locked doors, fenced-in school yards, locker searches and crisis drills—affects all children. The major consequences of violence and fear of violence are depression and anxiety, but additional effects include a sense of meaninglessness and emptiness; a loss of self-esteem and feelings of humiliation; a sense of impotence because of a perceived loss of control over various aspects of life; and a psychic numbing and emotional lethargy. Many children are experiencing sleep disturbances, irritability and excessive aggression. For others, action and decision-making seem difficult. For all children, the energy that is spent on survival is lost to academics.

The Changing Workforce

Less than a generation ago, the term "workforce" conjured up visions of white men dressed in either ties or blue shirts. By the turn of the next century, white males will comprise only 15 percent of the net additions to the labor force. The other 85 percent will be women and people from nonwhite and immigrant groups. This trend is reshaping both the color and cultural background of our workforce. Without training in learning to work cooperatively to achieve common goals among diverse groups of

STRAIGHT TALK

"I am writing in regards to an issue that has taken both the inner cities and suburbs by storm. It is scary, yet real. Being a sophomore in a suburban Jefferson County high school, I know the facts about violence in public schools. According to a recent survey taken by the National Education Association, every school day at least 100,000 students tote guns in schools, 160,000 skip classes because they fear physical harm, and 40 are hurt or killed by firearms . . . Action needs to be taken to help educate students about violence in their schools. When my parents were in school, all they had to worry about was an occasional fistfight. Now students everywhere are faced with the fear of attending their own school, no matter how 'nice' the school. I feel that with a little education and guidance, this ongoing problem will decrease. Although many people do not realize it, this violence shows no mercy. It could hit any school at any time."

LAURA TENFELDE, *age 15,*
in a letter to the editor
of the Courier-Journal, *Louisville, Kentucky, October 5, 1994*

people, linguistic and cultural problems between different ethnic and racial groups will be unavoidable.

At the same time, most companies face an extremely tight labor market as the baby bust of the 1960s and 1970s dramatically reduced the number of young people available to fill jobs. Yet that decreasing labor pool needs to become more highly qualified as our businesses face growing competitive pressures, an impossibility if our young people continue their path of alienation and early exit from our schools.

It is economic suicide to let our children fail, for any reason. They cannot be allowed to leave school without adequate knowledge of both academic and interpersonal skills. Whether or not educators have large minority populations in their schools, they

DID YOU KNOW?

At the end of the American Psychological Association's two-year study on violence and youth, they recommended the following specific violence reduction strategies:

- Early childhood interventions directed toward parents, child care providers and health care providers to help build the critical foundation of attitudes, knowledge and behavior related to aggression.
- School-based interventions to help schools provide a safe environment and effective programs to prevent violence.
- Heightened awareness of cultural diversity and involvement of community members in planning, implementing and evaluating intervention efforts.
- Development of the mass media's potential to be part of the solution to violence, not just a contributor to the problem.
- Limiting access to firearms by children and youth and teaching them how to prevent firearm violence.
- Reduction of youth involvement with alcohol and drugs, known contributing factors to violence by youth and to family violence directed at youth.
- Psychological health services for young perpetrators, victims and witnesses of violence to avert the trajectory toward later involvement in more serious violence.
- Education programs to reduce prejudice and hostility—two factors that lead to hate crimes and violence against social groups.
- Efforts to strengthen the ability of police and community leaders to prevent mob violence by early and appropriate intervention.

must think about the diversity of people with whom their students will come into contact throughout their lives. We must create school environments that retain students and teach them how to build respectful partnerships with those who are different from them.

STRATEGIES TO IMPROVE SCHOOL CULTURE

Children who stay in school, who feel good about it *and* good about their classmates, do so because their school is a safe and receptive environment for them, both physically and psychologically. There are certainly many factors in students' lives over which the schools have little or no control. But there are things educators *can* do to change the content and processes within our schools and improve the school climate to better serve this population. Adjusting the curriculum and other aspects of the educational structure to reflect the newest shifts in classroom composition are steps well taken toward assuring that students and families from all cultures who are already in the system, and

STRAIGHT TALK

"By the time children come to school, they have already learned very complex material as part of being socialized into their own culture. This means that in minority schooling we are dealing with a situation involving two cultures—the culture of the school and the culture of the child. When the two are not compatible, the school fails to teach, and the child fails to learn."

CATHIE JORDAN,
"Cultural Compatibility and the Education of Hawaiian Children: Implications for Mainland Educators," Educational Research Quarterly 8:4 (1984)

immigrants new to our country and our social structures, will have the skills to function together to build a peaceful future.

Multicultural Education

Just the mention of the term "multicultural education" immediately raises the hackles of some, educators and non-educators alike. Those who question the validity or necessity of multicultural education mistakenly assert that it is a curriculum that attempts to discount and replace all things traditional, an ineffective nod toward pluralism, an inappropriate outgrowth of the Civil Rights movement or simply a lame attempt at being "politically correct." Because of these uninformed indictments, multicultural education has been used, in some communities, as ammunition in the war between conservative and liberal groups. But multicultural education is not faction-specific, and it's important to understand the real goals of multicultural education, and the positive effects it can have on race relations *and* effective teaching.

Significant multicultural education, that which is integrated throughout all of the school curricula and practices, prepares children to live, learn and work together to achieve common goals in a culturally diverse world. Through multicultural education, children can:

- learn about and value the diversity that exists in the United States and throughout the world;
- become aware of and affirmed in their own cultural roots;
- understand the social, historical and psychological environments that cause people, including themselves, to think and behave as we do;
- become sensitive to other cultures and knowledgeable

about other viewpoints, and accurately assess similarities and differences among people of the world;

- understand their rights and responsibilities as citizens in a culturally pluralistic society;
- become adequately prepared to live fruitful lives in an increasingly global society with shifting and permeable borders.

Unfortunately, much of the current effort in multicultural education in the United States is directed at teaching students bits and pieces of information about other cultures—"products"—through monthly celebrations, cultural posters and world fairs. This additive approach can actually reinforce stereotypes by emphasizing exotic differences between people, and seems to be most often used in school systems where there are few minorities. But true multicultural education is not a field trip to Taco Bell, putting up a bulletin board about France, or having a conversation with a foreign student. Through a well-planned multicultural program, schools may be able to better prepare majority children for life in a pluralistic society while offering children of diverse cultures a sense of belonging that can make their school experiences more positive.

STRAIGHT TALK

"One of the biggest lies out here is that no matter what race or religion you are, it doesn't matter. Now, that's a lie, and we all know it. If we don't talk about these problems and take them on, they're going to get much, much worse."

SPIKE LEE

In order for multicultural education to be effective, curriculum design, textbooks and curricular materials must be bias-free and include ethnic and cultural content; there should be a commitment to providing inclusive in-school and extracurricular activities and parent-teacher councils; hiring practices ought to insure diverse staffing patterns and continuing support for minority teachers and staff; and teachers should receive adequate in-service training to provide them with information on how to make education multicultural.

We have both an opportunity and an obligation to use the wealth of our diversity—our stories, folk literature, art, music, as well as our experiences of poverty, discrimination and conflicts—to teach our children. Multicultural education is that type of education, and it can ultimately help all children to develop competencies they will need throughout their lives.

Human Rights Policies

On July 4, 1776, a document was signed by the Continental Congress that declared the United States an independent country. This statement of principles, the *Declaration of Independence,* subsequently became one of the most important legal and moral foundations for our country.

The second paragraph reads, "We hold these truths to be self-evident, that all men are created equal, that they are endowed by their Creator with certain unalienable Rights, that among these are Life, Liberty, and the pursuit of Happiness." Nowhere does it say, ". . . but not for *those* people."

A visible commitment to human rights within the school—a posted human rights policy statement, for example—is one of the most proactive approaches that a school can take to begin to insure that the diversity of the school community is not ignored, devalued or degraded.

Human rights policies need to state clear guidelines against any form of infringement upon the rights of others, such as racism or sexism. The policy must be well publicized not only to students and staff but to parents, too. Most important, the leadership of the school must be willing to follow through on their policies. They must be able to punish behavior that is counter to the policy as well as reward those in the school who actively promote human rights. Too often, acts of racism and other infringements of human rights are addressed only after the school staff has been asked repeatedly to take action. Whatever the reason, avoidance of human rights issues holds damaging consequences for students. First, because violations of human rights are strong, negative experiences for children, they draw students' attention away from academic pursuits. Second, because evasion of the issues sends signals to all students that racism and other forms of human rights violations are trivial concerns or, worse, that they are acceptable forms of behavior.

PROGRAMS THAT WORK

Kids Without Violence Program

The Kids Without Violence Program informs and educates parents, teachers, children and the general public about the processes by which kids are socialized to violence. It offers community and school-based programs that help children and adolescents examine the causes of and solutions to the violence that they may experience in their personal lives. Among its activities are the following:

- Promotion of public awareness that violence is a major public health issue affecting our nation's children.

(continued)

- Workshops on the socialization of children to violence, intended to promote positive responses to the problem.
- National information clearinghouse on the issue of youth violence.

For more information, contact

Dr. Richard J. Parker, Director
Kids Without Violence Program
(Affiliate of the Center on War & the Child)
P.O. Box 487
35 Benton Street
Eureka Springs, AR 72632
501-253-8900 phone

Resolving Conflict Creatively Program

Begun in 1985 as a collaborative effort of the New York City Public Schools and Educators for Social Responsibility, the Resolving Conflict Creatively Program (RCCP) has evolved into a highly effective partnership between a public and private agency and is now the largest program of its kind in the country. Its overall goals are as follows:

- To prepare educators to provide high quality instruction and effective school programs in conflict resolution and intergroup relations in a variety of settings across the country.

(continued)

- To transform the culture of participating schools so that they model values and principles of creative, nonviolent conflict resolution.

For more information, contact

Linda Lantieri, Director
RCCP National Center
163 Third Avenue, #103
New York, NY 10003
212-387-0025 phone 212-387-0510 fax

Violence Prevention Curriculum for Adolescents

This program is a ten-session course that addresses the growing problems of violence and homicide among young people. The curriculum package is based on the work of Dr. Deborah Prothrow-Stith, a physician at Boston City Hospital and an assistant professor at Boston University School of Medicine. The curriculum:

- Acknowledges anger as a normal and natural emotion.
- Provides hard-hitting facts that alert students to their high risk of being either the victim or the perpetrator of an act of violence.
- Offers positive ways to deal with anger and arguments, the leading precipitants of homicide.
- Allows students to analyze the precursors to a fight and to practice conflict resolution through role playing and videotaping.

(continued)

For more information, contact

EDC Publishing Center
Education Development Center, Inc.
55 Chapel Street
Newton, MA 02160
800-225-4276 phone   617-969-7100 phone

National Association for Mediation In Education

The National Association for Mediation in Education (NAME) promotes the development, implementation and institutionalization of school- and university-based conflict resolution programs and curricula. Since its founding in 1984, the organization has grown from a small, informal network of people interested in teaching students conflict resolution skills to the primary national and international clearinghouse for information, resources, technical assistance and training in the field of conflict resolution in education. Their services include publications, newsletter, conference, networking, technical assistance, research and referrals. Their goals include the following:

- Advancing the field of conflict resolution.
- Promoting an appreciation for diversity and building skills to deal constructively with our differences.
- Establishing and sustaining school-based conflict resolution programs.
- Continuing development as a national organization capable of leadership in advancing the field.

(continued)

- Undertaking fund-raising and resource development activities.

For more information contact:

NAME
205 Hampshire House
Box 33635
University of Massachusetts
Amherst, MA 01003-3635
413-545-2462 phone
413-545-4802 fax
name @ acad.umass.edu e-mail

Hopkins County, Kentucky, Policy on Race Relations, Ethnic Relations and Multiculturalism

Mission Statement:
To promote a positive climate in each Hopkins County school, which is conducive to every student earning a quality education and being prepared for a life in a society composed of many different cultural, racial and ethnic strands.

The following comprises the fifteen-point policy presently in force in the Hopkins County, Kentucky, schools:

1. The Hopkins County Board of Education is committed to the belief that all doctrines and practices of racial and/or ethnic superiority are morally reprehensible

(continued)

and socially destructive. Such practices will not be accepted in the school system.

2. The Hopkins County Board of Education condemns and does not tolerate any expression of racial or cultural bias by its staff and students.

3. The Hopkins County Board of Education assumes the responsibility in the elimination of all racial and cultural discrimination, including those policies and practices which, while not intentionally discriminatory, have a discriminatory effect.

4. The Hopkins County Board of Education reaffirms its commitment to develop and promote racial harmony among its students, staff and the community and to provide education that is antiracist and multicultural.

5. The Hopkins County Board of Education assigns high priority to its policy on race relations, ethnic relations and multiculturalism and commits itself to the implementation and ongoing evaluation of this policy.

6. The Hopkins County Board of Education will continue to develop curricular and co-curricular programs that provide the opportunities for students to acquire positive attitudes toward racial, cultural and religious diversity.

7. The Hopkins County Board of Education will attempt to ensure that all curricula, textbooks, audiovisual and other resource materials used in Hopkins County schools are free from stereotypes based on race or culture.

8. The Hopkins County Board of Education will attempt to ensure that schools in their day-to-day operations and co-curricular activities identify and eliminate those policies and practices which, while not intentionally discriminatory, have a discriminatory effect.

(continued)

9. The Hopkins County Board of Education recognizes that in order to ensure equal access and an opportunity for the achievement of their full potential, students from racial and cultural minority groups may require special consideration with respect to
   A. reception,
   B. assessment,
   C. placement,
   D. programming,
   E. monitoring, and
   F. meaningful communications with parents/guardians.

10. The Hopkins County Board of Education provides encouragement and opportunities for all staff to develop their knowledge, sensitivity and skills in areas related to multiculturalism, race relations and antiracist education.

11. The Hopkins County Board of Education condemns and refuses to tolerate all manifestations of discrimination on the basis of race, ethnicity, culture or religion by its students and staff and will take an active role in their elimination.

12. The Hopkins County Board of Education commits itself to the development and maintenance of practices designed to eliminate and/or prevent discriminatory barriers in the workplace.

13. The Hopkins County Board of Education is committed to the full and meaningful participation of the multiracial and multicultural community in the life of its schools.

(continued)

14. The Hopkins County Board of Education, in cooperation with other groups, facilitates the development of mutual awareness, understanding and appreciation among all racial, religious and cultural groups.

15. The Hopkins County Board of Education recognizes each individual's inherent right of freedom of expression, and reinforces the Board's right to require conformance to its policies both during working hours and in the case of any conduct outside the work environment that would impact negatively on the school system.

Conflict Resolution Programs

Conflict is a daily reality for everyone, whether at home or at school. Society is structured so that some individuals have more power and control than others, and the conflict that results is a natural phenomenon.

Children, too, need to work out their feelings about power and control. The problem is the increasing levels of aggression they're using to "resolve" conflicts.

Children develop their own personal strategies for dealing with conflict based on what they see and learn. Given their general lack of awareness of nonviolent alternatives for resolving conflicts, how do we help them swap a combative attitude for a cooperative one? The Centers for Disease Control in Atlanta, Georgia, has declared that violence has reached epidemic proportions, and urges that nonviolent conflict resolution be taught to all students from preschool through twelfth grade, to counteract that violence.

Conflict resolution training, included as a legitimate part of their curriculum, can offer children a significant opportunity to

develop some of the most important social skills an individual can possess: on the
cognitive level, the understanding that conflict is a normal part of everyday life, and
on the behavioral level, the
ability to resolve conflict nonviolently.

A meaningful program al-
lows children to study the
causes of conflict, the different styles that people use to
deal with anger and conflict,
the process through which
conflict escalates and the
skills needed to manage and
resolve conflict creatively and

STRAIGHT TALK

"Classrooms are a wonderful place
to start preventing violence. Kids
go home and bring this new
approach to their families, but
we are asking kids to do the
impossible unless we also deal
with changing the larger picture:
the ethos of the school and
neighborhood, in a culture that
glorifies violent heroes. Otherwise,
kids will master conflict resolution
skills that no one values."

DR. DEBORAH PROTHROW-STITH,
Assistant Dean,
Harvard School of Public Health

nonviolently. Children can explore conflict in a nurturing and
cooperative classroom environment, through a number of different situations and perspectives. Through this type of program,
they learn valuable life skills—verbal and nonverbal communication, listening, problem solving, critical thinking, decision-
making and negotiation—and ultimately develop a productive
response to conflict that helps build peaceful relationships in
their classrooms, schools and communities.

Typically we think of these skills as chiefly useful to adults.
But it's essential for several reasons that we redirect our efforts
toward children. First, our eagerness as adults to intercede in
children's fights sends an implied message to them that we see
them as incapable of settling their own disputes. But even the
smallest children *can* understand many elements of arriving at
outcomes where both sides win. Second, children take into their

adulthood the sense of self that they create in their childhood. It is during childhood that they form their worldviews, as well as their methods of dealing with frustration and conflict. If they learn as children that dealing with conflict in violent, combative ways is the prevalent method, they will carry that impression into their adulthood. If, instead, they learn as children a wide range of positive methods to resolve conflict peacefully, in ways that are appealing and matched to their level of development, they can spend less of their time as adults undoing destructive habits and more time contributing to society.

Cross-Cultural Counseling

As our schools address their urgent mission of helping prepare every child for life in a diverse society, the school counselor can be one of the most important links in the system. And as much as anyone in that system, counselors need to be aware of both the present reality and the direction of the future if they are to help children move more easily into a world filled with ever increasing change.

But counseling is primarily a white middle-class activity. And its practitioners are trained in Euro-centered counseling programs which encompass Western-oriented philosophical assumptions. For example, the dominant culture of most schools requires that students take a major role in coun-

---

STRAIGHT TALK

"Education of minority students is synonymous with continued economic security for the nation."

JUDY SCHRAG,
*Director of the Office
of Special Education Programs
in the Office of Special Education
and Rehabilitative Services,
Department of Education,
Washington, DC*

seling sessions. Most Asian Americans, Hispanics and Native Americans, however, may have trouble with this—having been raised to assume their positions within clearly defined traditional roles which include deference to their elders. Therefore, a minority student who is asked to initiate conversation may become uneasy and tense, and respond with only short phrases or statements. The counselor could interpret this behavior as negative when it may actually be a sign of respect.

In order to work successfully with minority students, counselors must take into account each student's worldview, show respect for his or her history and be as unbiased as possible. This requires counselors to learn new techniques and acquire new skills for understanding, motivating and empowering each individual student regardless of race, gender, religion or creed. At the same time, counselors must also be aware of the fact that the parameters of culture extend far beyond racial and ethnic categories.

To guide students effectively in a multicultural environment, a culturally sensitive counselor will consider these major points:

- The historical perspectives and the social support systems of diverse families.
- The unique characteristics of the value systems of diverse families.
- Any cultural communication barriers, either verbal or nonverbal, that may hinder the level of trust between the student and the counselor.
- The development of innovative treatment strategies based on cultural considerations. These should build a sense of personal worth in students, empowering them as both individuals within their particular cultural context and as an integral part of the larger school/community culture.

The degree to which counseling contributes to the development of a student's concept of her human potential is clear. All children in our schools today must receive the support and motivation they need to identify and achieve their goals, regardless of their past histories, their present situations or the sometimes limited expectations we hold for their futures.

The "melting pot" analogy that has been so prevalent in this country for generations is no longer appropriate. We are, in fact, in a superb position to benefit from the knowledge that comes from experiencing a confluence of cultures. Our schools must play an essential role in preparing our children for life in this diverse, complex and interdependent world.

HOW DO YOU RATE?

Checklist for Cross-Cultural Counseling

YES NO

☐ ☐ Do I try to see the world of the student through his eyes?

☐ ☐ Does the student realize that I share perceptions with her?

☐ ☐ Am I warm, compassionate and interested in the student? Do I demonstrate this in the way I address the student?

☐ ☐ Are there certain things that I am reluctant to say to the student, and if so, what implications does that inhibition have on our relationship?

☐ ☐ On what important issues do the values, beliefs and opinions of the student vary from mine? Are those differences influencing my ability to accept him?

WHAT DOES IT MEAN?

At-Risk Student Population

Those children who perform below expectation levels and who experience one or more social, health, educational or developmental problems that interfere with learning and place them at risk in their school experiences. They may show one or more of these characteristics:

- Perform below the national average
- Display poor attendance patterns
- Show a lack of identification with school
- Experience discipline problems
- Have verbal deficiencies
- Show low perceptual performance
- Have low socioeconomic status
- Have low self-esteem
- Fail to see relevance of education to life experiences
- Experience family problems
- Experience early and chronic school failure due to lack of achievement in basic skills

WHAT YOU CAN DO

Multicultural Education

- Develop and implement board or school policy that improves the district's or school's multicultural perspective.

- Check district and school procedures, practices, curriculum guides and lesson plans to be sure they are free of bias.

- Review textbooks now in use in terms of the criteria presented by the policy. Discontinue the use of those publications that fall short of these standards.

- Overcome in part the multicultural inadequacies of some texts by using other instructional materials that more nearly meet the standards stated in the policy.

- Insure that students use more recent editions of social studies texts.

- Develop strategies to increase the number of minority teachers in your school or district.

- Integrate minority- and racism-related content into the curriculum throughout the school year rather than setting aside a "Black History Week" or "Women's History Week."

- Make sure that the contributions, feelings and lifestyles of

---

STRAIGHT TALK

"If we are to achieve a richer culture, rich in contrasting values, we must recognize the whole gamut of human potentialities, and so weave a less arbitrary social fabric, one in which each diverse human gift will find a fitting place."

MARGARET MEAD,
Sex and Temperament in Three Primitive Societies, 1935

minorities are represented throughout the curriculum all year long.

Multicultural education should start with a child's earliest school experiences. In the early grades:

- Listen for opportunities to confront students' misconceptions, such as misinformation about skin color, respecting the child's limited awareness.
- Because colors such as black and brown are often associated with darkness or evil, counteract negative associations with positive perspectives.
- Introduce children to multicultural children's books in story hours, in book discussion groups and in developing curriculum for whole language reading. Look for authentic literature.
- Seek hands-on variety by using diverse play props such as chopsticks, woks and clay pots in the housekeeping area, and tangrams and abacuses in the math area, and by integrating the doll collection.

DID YOU KNOW?

The Literature We Teach

In a recent study of secondary schools, the National Center on Literature Teaching and Learning determined the following:

- Of the 11,579 individual selections reported in the public school sample, 81 percent were by male authors, 98

(continued)

percent were by white (non-Hispanic) authors, and 99 percent were written within the United States, United Kingdom or Western European tradition.

- In spite of efforts to broaden the canon over the past several decades, the study found only marginal increases in the percentage of selections written by women (from 17 percent in 1963 to 19 percent in 1988) or by writers from alternative cultural traditions (from 0.6 percent in 1963 to 2 percent in 1988).

(Source: Applebee, Arthur N. "Stability and Change in the High School Canon," *English Journal* 8:1 (September 1992), pp. 27–32.)

HOW DO YOU RATE?

Checklist for Multicultural Education

YES NO

☐   ☐   Do you believe that all children have the capacity to learn?

☐   ☐   Do you try regularly to expose students to other cultures?

☐   ☐   Does your classroom show evidence of the involvement of the teacher and students in learning about various cultures?

(continued)

YES NO

☐ ☐ Have you approached representative members of each culture in your classroom and asked their assistance in providing information regarding that culture?

☐ ☐ Does the formal curriculum, and all of the textbooks and other teaching materials, include, visually and in the text, members of the students' groups and a range of other cultural groups?

☐ ☐ Does the school culture and the hidden curriculum (bulletin boards, cultural staffing patterns and so on) reflect racial and cultural diversity? Does it convey the belief that being different does not mean being deficient?

☐ ☐ Do the school board and the administrators have an effective plan for infusion of multicultural education that they communicate to faculty, support staff, students and parents?

☐ ☐ Do you offer factual, realistic and balanced treatment of the past and present?

☐ ☐ Are all teaching materials free of stereotypes, presenting accurate, multidimensional pictures of cultural groups?

☐ ☐ Do you know where in the school or district to get information and assistance with planning appropriate multicultural instruction and activities?

(continued)

YES NO

☐ ☐ Do you take staff development courses to help you increase your effectiveness in making your teaching multicultural?

☐ ☐ Can each of your students see in her classroom a picture or some other visual image of someone with whom she can identify?

☐ ☐ Do your students know why and how cultures come into being?

☐ ☐ Do they understand point of view and multiple perspectives?

PROGRAMS THAT WORK

Words and Music

For almost two decades, the successful Words and Music program of the Country Music Hall of Fame and Museum has offered students in the Nashville, Tennessee, area an opportunity to expand their creative writing and music skills. Using themselves and their families as subjects for their songs, and with the help of professional songwriters, students in this classroom program are introduced to the songwriting process through the basic elements of a language arts curriculum, while at the same time exploring their heritage.

For more information, contact:

(continued)

John Knowles
The Country Music Hall of Fame and Museum
A Division of the Country Music Foundation
4 Music Square East
Nashville, TN 37203
(615) 256-1639 phone
(615) 255-2245 fax

National Council for the Traditional Arts

Founded in 1933, The National Council for the Traditional Arts is dedicated to the presentation and documentation of American folk arts and is the oldest multicultural producing and presenting organization in the United States. Their programs celebrate and honor arts that are deeply traditional—music, crafts, stories and dance passed down from generation to generation—and are available to the public through concerts, tours, festivals, radio and television programs, films and other venues. They are a rich resource for teachers interested in bringing our country's traditions into the classroom.

For more information, contact:

The National Council for the Traditional Arts
1320 Fenwick Lane
Suite 200
Silver Spring, MD 20910
301-565-0654 phone
301-565-0472 fax

UPDATE REPORT

The following acts of legislation have resulted in the formulation of programs on the federal level that can be considered supportive of multicultural education:

- *Title IX of the Elementary and Secondary Education Act of 1965 (ESEA)*
  The Ethnic Heritage Program emerged from ESEA and has funded projects that focus on ethnicity.
- *Title IV of the Civil Rights Act of 1964*
  This act provides technical and financial assistance to desegregating school systems when requested.
- *Title VII of the Emergency School Aid Act of 1972*
  This act was designed to meet the needs of students and faculty that have resulted from discrimination and group isolation.
- *Title VII of the Elementary and Secondary Education Act*
  The emphasis of this piece of legislation is on language; it is known as the Bilingual Education Act. This act provides assistance to programs that are designed to address language differences.
- *Title IX of the 1972 Education Amendments*
  This act prohibits discrimination on the basis of sex in federally assisted educational programs or activities.

FOR YOUR INFORMATION

Multicultural References

Following are some references that may be of particular help in infusing your curriculum with multicultural content:

The Before Columbus Foundation Fiction Anthology: Selections from the American Book Awards 1980–1990
Ishmael Reed, Kathryn Trueblood and Shawn Wong, editors

W.W. Norton & Company
1992
ISBN 0-3933-0832-4

Braided Lives: An Anthology of Multicultural American Writing
Deborah Appleman and Margaret Reed, Cochairs, Editorial Board
Minnesota Humanities Commission
1991
ISBN 0-9629-2980-8

Children's Literature: Springboard to Understanding the Developing World
Jerry Diakiw, Project Director
UNICEF Canada
1988
ISBN 0-9215-6403-1

Helping Kids Learn Multi-Cultural Concepts: A Handbook of Strategies
Michael G. Pasternak
Research Press Company
1979
ISBN 0-8782-2194-8

The Latino Experience in U.S. History
(part of a series which includes the African American experience and
    other ethnic and racial groups)
Globe Book Company
1992
ISBN 0-1301-9969-9

*Making Waves: An Anthology of Writings By and About Asian American
    Women*
Asian Women United of California, editors
Beacon Press
1989
ISBN 0-8070-5905-6

Multicultural America: A Resource Book for Teachers of Humanities and American Studies
Betty E. M. Ch'maj, editor
University Press of America
1993
ISBN 0-8191-8917-O

Multicultural Holidays
Julia Jasmine
Teacher Created Materials, Inc.
1994
ISBN 1-5573-4615-1

The Multicultural Workshop: A Reading and Writing Program
Books 1 and 2
Linda Lonon Blanton and Linda Lee
Heinle & Heinle Publishers
1994
ISBN 0-8384-4834-8 and 0-8384-4835-6

Peace Tales: World Folktales to Talk About
Margaret Read Macdonald
Linnet Books
1992
ISBN 0-2080-2329-1

Spider Woman's Granddaughters: Traditional Tales and Contemporary Writing by Native American Women
Paula Gunn Allen, editor
Ballantine Books
1989
ISBN 0-4499-0508-X

Turning On Learning: Five Approaches for Multicultural Teaching Plans for Race, Class, Gender, and Disability
Carl A. Grant and Christine E. Sleeter
Macmillan Publishing Company
1989
ISBN 0-675-20805-X

Unwinding Threads: Writing by Women in Africa
Charlotte H. Bruner, editor
Heinemann International
1983
ISBN 0-4359-0256-3

FOR YOUR INFORMATION

Multicultural Periodicals

These three are exceptionally helpful for educators in addressing multicultural issues:

Teaching Tolerance
Published by the Southern Poverty Law Center, this magazine is rich with practical ideas for the classroom and is free for the asking.
For subscription information, contact:
Teaching Tolerance
400 Washington Ave.
Montgomery, AL 36104

Rethinking Schools
This is an independent journal that is fiercely committed to issues of equity and social justice, and is written by teachers, parents and educational activists.

For subscription information, contact:
Rethinking Schools
1001 E. Keefe Avenue
Milwaukee, WI 53212
414-964-9646 phone
414-964-7220 fax

Multicultural Review
The Review is a monthly magazine intended to provide reviews of multicultural materials and information on the subject of multiculturalism.
For subscription information, contact:
Multicultural Review
Greenwood Publishing Group, Inc.
88 Post Road West
P.O. Box 5007
Westport, CT 06881-5007

FOR YOUR INFORMATION

Culturgrams: The Nations Around Us

Volume I: The Americas and Europe
Volume II: Africa, Asia and Oceania
To help teachers relate to immigrant or migrant students in their classrooms, and to help build better bridges of understanding with people all over the world, the David Kennedy Center for International Studies at Brigham Young University has developed a series of four-page summaries of customs, values, traditions and lifestyles of more than 120 different countries. While they don't claim to produce experts on a country or its people, they do give a quick overview of each country which can assist teach-

ers in gaining first insights into the cultures from which their students come.

$90.00 per set ($45 each) for profit-making organizations
$60.00 per set ($30 each) for not-for-profit organizations

For more information, contact:

Garrett Park Press
P.O. Box 190 F
Garrett Park, MD 20896
301-946-2553 phone
301-949-8173 fax

Positive School Climate

- Make sure that the school is student-centered—that students are the primary focus in the school. Promote and sustain social, teaching and learning structures in which all children experience success regardless of race, ethnicity, gender, socioeconomic status or other areas of difference.
- Have the culture of the school reflect and value the cultures of the students. Legitimize and affirm the history, contributions, values and perspectives of the cultural groups to which students belong by integrating them into the school.
- Show organizational health and that the school is being "led" and not simply "managed." Encourage a strong belief on the part of everyone in the school that he can and does make a difference in the lives of his students.
- Provide opportunities for teacher and student dialogue, and allow input from both teachers and students to the development and maintenance of academic and social goals and procedures.

- Provide opportunities for children to discuss openly why they react positively or negatively toward a particular cultural group.
- Teach children about the processes by which people develop stereotypes and have them identify ways in which they have seen themselves follow those processes.
- Address the multiple components that reinforce one another across the students' everyday social contexts: family, school, peer groups, exposure to media and community.

HOW DO YOU RATE?

Checklist for Rating Your School Climate

YES NO

☐ ☐ Do your staff members use language that is free from racial, ethnic and sexual slurs at all times?

☐ ☐ Is it acceptable for staff and students to talk about cultural differences?

☐ ☐ Is the comfort level in the school such that staff and students communicate freely with those who are different from them? Can these contacts be initiated by either person?

☐ ☐ Can the staff accurately identify the major demographic groups within the school and identify traditional modes of learning that are valued within each of those groups?

(continued)

YES NO

☐ ☐ Does your school or district have a policy that explicitly condemns racially, sexually and ethnically biased behavior?

☐ ☐ Does that policy have clear complaint reporting, fact finding and appeal procedures?

☐ ☐ Are consequences for violating this policy clearly stated and regularly enforced?

☐ ☐ Does the planning for all school events, awards and programs reflect the diversity of people in the school?

☐ ☐ Are mascots, emblems, team names and trophies free from racial, gender and ethnic bias?

☐ ☐ Are there important events and celebrations in the school that emphasize human unity and diversity, such as Earth Day and United Nations Day?

☐ ☐ Do important events and celebrations reflect the heritage of people other than male European Americans?

☐ ☐ Do pictures, decorations and ornaments in the school reflect the diversity of its population and emphasize the message of unity and diversity?

☐ ☐ Does your school have a plan for improving intergroup relations?

(continued)

YES NO

☐   ☐   Has there been recognition and support for the formal and informal leaders of the school community who promote positive intergroup relations?

☐   ☐   Have you talked about cultural influences on teaching and learning with colleagues who are of a different race, gender or ethnicity than you?

☐   ☐   Have you thought about how your own culturally influenced teaching and learning styles are perceived by colleagues and students who are different from you?

☐   ☐   Do you honestly believe that all students are capable of succeeding, regardless of their racial or ethnic group and gender?

Multicultural Counseling

- Establish a personal relationship with each student. Learn what special needs each of your students has and make sure that the students know you care enough to help them in any way that you can.

- Teach your students to set up a personal support network. Have them write down three favorite teachers and three favorite friends in the school whom they would trust if they needed them. Have them research community resources that are there to assist them, such as hot lines, teen health clinics and youth service centers. Have them each complete a personal support network chart with names and phone numbers of resources that appeal to them. Make sure a copy is kept by you and each of them.

- Try to meet individually with each of your most at-risk students at least once a week. It may mean chatting for a few minutes at the end of a class, meeting for a few quick moments in the hall or getting together during their lunch period.

STRAIGHT TALK

"As individuals we only have a little power, but the power that we have is profound nevertheless: it is the power to care."

DR. DEBORAH PROTHROW-STITH, Deadly Consequences: How Violence Is Destroying Our Teenage Population, 1994

- Understand your students' vocabulary and do not be afraid to ask for definitions and explanations.

- The resources of your school and community should be used to supplement and enhance the efforts of each other. Actively cooperate with—and initiate if you have to—local community support services for children.

- Find out which of your most at-risk students are participating in extracurricular activities and if their families are attending. If you sense the need, attend one or two of their events.

- Talk with students and other members of culturally diverse communities to expand your own knowledge of different cultures. Spend time as a participant and observer at their events and, if possible, in their homes.

- Consider the value of cultural differences between nonwhite Americans and other ethnic groups and how your own personal values influence the way you guide students. Consider the ways your personal values influence the way you view both the presenting problem and the goals for your counseling sessions.

- Understand how verbal and nonverbal communication make your students uncomfortable because of cultural differences in styles of communicating.
- Be aware that in the event of a tragedy as a result of community or school violence, children will need grief counseling. They will need to be told what happened quietly, simply and directly. Avoid using platitudes or religious symbolism. Answer all questions directly and honestly, but avoid unnecessary details. Remember that there is no one "correct" response to grief.

Human Rights

- Remember that you are a model. Students will often follow your lead, and the ambience in the classroom is determined in part by the way you handle the relationships among them. Assess how you interpret the behavior of both minority and white students. One way to do this is to invite a friendly and honest colleague to observe your classroom interaction and give you informal feedback.
- Formalize a program that includes human rights training for students and staff; standardizing procedures for handling infractions of human rights; providing leadership and coordination of all human rights matters in the school.
- Infuse the curriculum and instructional program with a human rights perspective,
- Do not tolerate the telling of racist or ethnic jokes. Be mindful that many local, state and federal laws covering workplace discrimination consider the telling of racial or ethnic jokes to be proof of discrimination.

CHAPTER FOUR

Growing Up Equal: Gender Fairness in the Classroom

More than two decades have passed since Congress prohibited sex discrimination in education by passing Title IX of the Educational Amendments. Yet stereotyping by sex and its sister corollary—gender bias in education—continue to create a 51 percent majority of second-class citizens.

EARLY GENDER SOCIALIZATION

Parents' gender role expectations shape their children's behavior from birth. Babies in blue diapers are often characterized by adults as active and loud; those in pink are described as quiet and sweet; and those in yellow so confuse observers that many ask about the sex of a child in order to know how to treat it.

Infant girls are usually touched and talked to more by their mothers, while baby boys are encouraged to explore and play independently. The children learn early that the two genders have different territories: a special room or chair is set aside for the use of the men, while the women's places—the kitchen, for example—are usually public and open to invasion.

Even very young children are often unconsciously encouraged to embrace sex-stereotyped roles through their toys and games. Through their action toys and building kits, boys learn about three-dimensional structures, velocity and math concepts which become a solid foundation of their practical knowledge. Girls are prompted to express themselves verbally, and learn to explain with words processes they cannot "see." Stereotypic storybook characters and language, different methods of disciplining, separate treatment in activities involving risks, emphasis on physical appearance for girls, divergent expectations regarding assertiveness in social interactions, and peer pressure to conform to stereotypic images all contribute to the control of a girl's alternatives and, more importantly, her motivation to choose. By the time school begins, many children have spent five years at home where their parents and others have telegraphed alarm if the male children haven't developed their tendencies to be "all boy," and the girls theirs to be feminine.

> ### STRAIGHT TALK
>
> "If we teach *today's* students to live in *tomorrow's* world with *yesterday's* rules, we may as well send them to explore the ocean floor without oxygen. Unarmed with skills and knowledge and unaware of their options, they may be overcome before they even begin."
>
> A-GAY-YAH: A Gender Equity Curriculum for Grades Six through Twelve, *American Indian Resource Center, Tahlequah, Oklahoma, 1992*

SEXISM IN THE SCHOOL

Once children enter school, the hidden curriculum—unbalanced staffing patterns, unequal distribution of power and authority within the school, invisibility of women in curricular materials—maintains and extends this socialization pattern. There is no shortage in most schools of role models—most leadership positions are held by men—to indicate to girls that, in many areas, education is a spectator sport.

Girls in Math and Science

As we near the turn of the century, science and business leaders are expressing increasing concern about the projected shortages of scientific and technical personnel. Their anxieties are justified: Our nation's economic and political vitality is directly linked to our ability to enlarge the talent pool of students planning careers in math, science and technology. Since more than two-thirds of new entrants into the labor force will be women and minorities by the year 2000, why are barriers still erected which prevent more girls from gaining the skills they need to enter these critical careers?

Research indicates that despite little difference in gender achievement in math and science in the lower grades, the success levels of girls in these areas begins a steady decline once they enter middle school. By the age of seventeen, boys score considerably higher on tests in these subjects.

Aside from early gender socialization that denies girls experience and skills in problem solving through the use of tools and mechanical objects, they face other forms of discouragement that prevent them from fulfilling their potential. Why girls find math, science and technology achievement elusive results from a number of factors:

- Most math curricula in the early grades focus on interactive memorization ability; many girls achieve at that point because they arrive at school with those skills. Boys regularly receive remediation to help them develop and improve those capacities in the early years. In middle school, the focus shifts to higher order, abstract concepts that depend on spatial visualization and other skills with which boys come to school. There is no parallel shift in remediation. Girls are not generally encouraged to develop their higher order math skills in the same way that boys were assisted in the early grades. Consequently, girls are less likely to persevere and extend their math education, and most either take more rudimentary courses or drop the subject altogether.

- Evidence shows that boys and girls approach learning from different perspectives and employ different learning styles. Most girls prefer to use a conversational style that cultivates group accord, a process through which ideas build on one another. Boys learn through argument, individual activity and independent work, skills they learn early on. Their classroom style of public debate, in which they challenge one another in order to learn, is in direct opposition to the learning style of girls, in which mutual support and the building of collaborative knowledge are fundamental aspects. Yet the mainstream model of education in math, science and technology classes supports the learning styles of boys and leaves out a large percentage of the learning community, including girls, whose learning styles are neither recognized nor affirmed.

- Sex-biased career counseling often prevents girls from getting information about career possibilities requiring competence in advanced mathematics or science. Nor are they regularly exposed to role models of women who are engaged in successful math or science careers.
- Parents of many girls involuntarily fail to provide support for their daughters' interest in math or science.
- Girls frequently believe that math and science have no relevance in their lives.

Even computers, frequently cited as the vehicle for overcoming a wide array of inequities, have not been used equally:

- Computer science is often narrowly identified with mathematics, which reinforces its stereotype as being a discipline that is more accessible to boys.
- Lack of equipment and software in schools has led, in many cases, to scheduling patterns that limit use of computers to those students who exhibit more success in using them rather than to the slower or more average students. Setting difficult prerequisites for computer courses, and even for the use of the school's computers, also deprives average and slower students of computer opportunities.
- Software that incorporates stereotypes further reinforces girls' negative attitude toward computer science.

Gender Teaching

How children are taught is at least as important as *what* they are taught. Teachers are often unaware of how aspects of their behavior communicate expectations that can easily derail girls' academic achievement.

Children's success in school is related to the amount as well as the type of attention they receive from their teachers, regardless of whether the attention is negative or positive. Studies have found that males receive more attention from the teacher than do females in classrooms from preschool to the university. More attention is paid to boys by teachers who do the following:

- Expect boys to work more independently, ask them higher order questions and criticize them more for misbehavior, even when they are acting no worse than the girls.
- Call directly on boys more than girls.
- Recognize boys more when they volunteer in class.
- Pay less attention when girls speak.
- Nod and gesture more in response to boys.
- Give more patronizing or impatient responses to girls.
- Allow girls to be interrupted more by other students and physically "squeezed out" by boys in the laboratory, computer room, in demonstration projects and on field trips.
- Assume that assertive and direct boys are more knowledgeable than hesitant, polite or shy girls.
- Underestimate the competence of girls, especially minority girls.
- Get to know boys informally more than girls.

The surprising fact is that not only do boys demand more attention, but teachers of both sexes actively solicit their responses more than those of girls!

The recent pioneering studies on gender bias in schools conducted by Myra and David Sadker and the investigation into gender teaching by the American Association of University Women show that what people once assumed to be innate gender differences are in fact produced by adults' different behavior toward boys and girls, behavior of which most adults are unaware. The studies show that these subtle classroom behaviors contribute to girls' tendency to lose interest in the school and career tracks traditionally associated with boys. They also show that the demands on women and men in the workforce are very different from what they were even a generation ago, and that gender-stereotypic responses to boys and girls are detrimental to both sexes.

Boys Are Affected by Gender Bias, Too

What has not been acknowledged until very recently is the degree to which gender-stereotyping and gender bias limits males as well as females. Sex role socialization subordinates people to preconceived, limiting forms of conduct, academic achievement and employment regardless of personal strengths, motivation and professional or vocational dreams.

In the case of men, some of these stereotypes are actually life-threatening. The indicators of physical and psychological trauma men experience in order to achieve, acquire prestige and money and prove their manhood are becoming well known. Being a man, for many, is a high-risk lifestyle that places extraordinary demands on their health and happiness:

- The annual death rate for cancer is nearly one-and-a-half times higher for men than for women.
- Death rates from heart disease are twice as high in men as in women.
- The ratio of ulcers in men versus women is two to one.
- Within a few years of divorce, the divorced men's death rate is three times the death rate for divorced women.
- Men are four times more likely than women to be the victims of murder.
- Men are the victims of on-the-job accidents at a rate at least six times higher than that for women.
- Men in the United States can expect to live an average of eight years less than women.

No one is immune to the subtle pressures of sex role socialization. As boys and girls prepare for life in an adult world, neither is convincingly provided the option to be and do what he or she wants to be and do.

SEXUAL HARASSMENT

Another gender-related and growing problem that can undermine the effectiveness of schooling for both boys and girls is sexual harassment. Several factors complicate this issue, including the pervasive uncertainty about just what constitutes sexual harassment; the fact that males and females have different perspectives on the issue; and that each case will vary based on the facts and the relationship between the parties.

DID YOU KNOW?

Parents and educators can examine their own feelings by discussing their responses to the following situations:

- At seven years, she says she intends to be President.
- At ten, she wants to try out for the school's soccer team.
- At twelve, she wants to be an engineer.
- At fourteen, she wants to take shop class.
- At fifteen, she is asking about union apprenticeships.
- At sixteen, she wants to go to MIT and plans to be president of General Motors.
- At seventeen, she says she has decided to go to business school so she can get a job right away and work and save money so she can get married, because that's what her boyfriend wants.

What are your responses to her? What resources can you point out? What courses would you suggest? Read the list again and use "he" as the reference. Does that change your feelings and your response?
(Source: *Teacher Skill Guide for Combating Sexism: Module #5, Fostering Independence*, Education Development Center, Newton, MA, 1979.)

The law regarding sexual harassment is based on Title VII of the Civil Rights Act of 1964 and Title IX of the 1972 Educational Amendments. Guidelines from the Equal Employment Opportunity Commission (EEOC) can serve as a starting point in understanding this sometimes clouded issue:

Sexual harassment refers to unwelcome sexual advances, requests for sexual favors, and other verbal or physical conduct of a sexual nature when (1) submission to such conduct is made either explicitly or implicitly a term or condition of one's employment, (2) submission to or rejection of such conduct is used as a basis for an employment decision, or (3) such conduct has the purpose or effect of substantially interfering with one's work performance or creating an intimidating, hostile, or offensive work environment.

In a landmark case, *Meritor Savings Bank, FSB* v. *Vinson* (1986), the Supreme Court said that for claims of sexual harassment based on a "hostile environment" to be actionable, they must be sufficiently severe or pervasive to alter the conditions of the victim's employment and create an abusive working environment. Sexual harassment, however, need not involve conduct that is explicitly sexual in nature but may include "any harassment or unequal treatment of an employee or group of employees that would not occur but for the sex of the employee or employees" (*McKinney* v. *Dole* [1985]).

Although most sexual harassment cases occur in the general workforce, the courts have stated that there is no substantial distinction between the work environment and the school environment that would prohibit sexual harassment in the former while accepting it in the latter. Therefore, school personnel—including superintendents, principals, administrators and other supervisory staff, and teachers—can be liable and held responsible in sexual harassment lawsuits for their own harassing activities and for their failure to address claims of sexual harassment by others for whom they are responsible.

Sexual harassment, of course, is not limited to the adult

population. In fact, according to the survey conducted by the American Association of University Women and described in their report "Hostile Hallways—The AAUW Survey on Sexual Harassment in America's Schools (June 1993)," it is an experience common to the vast majority of eighth- to eleventh-grade students in America's public schools, often begins several grades earlier and is on the rise in both middle and high schools.

Exposure to sexual harassment can negatively affect the emotional, social and physical sense of well-being of both girls and boys. Some victims describe feelings similar to those identified by rape victims. Other reactions expressed by victims of sexual harassment are anger, frustration, depression, anxiety and a sense of self-blame, any of which can further cause a decrease in the ability to concentrate, high absenteeism and a severe drop in learning potential.

Rather than view the increase in complaints and reported cases of sexual harassment with the urgency it deserves, however, many school administrators continue to treat the incidents as harmless. But like any other infraction of human rights, this lack of serious attention to a serious problem sends a clear message of tacit approval to children, girls in particular. And along with that message comes another informal, yet crystal clear bit of information: that school, or at least those classes where they are most likely to be harassed, are not places for them.

THE CALL FOR EQUITY

Just as all aspects of the school are potential carriers of damaging race and ethnic-oriented messages, they are also potential carriers of equally damaging, implicit or explicit gender-oriented com-

DID YOU KNOW?

Sexual Harassment Survey

These are some findings from a survey commissioned by the American Association of University Women's Education Foundation, conducted by Louis Harris and Associates in 1993:

- Sexual harassment affects four out of every five teenagers in schools nationwide, but few victims report it.
- Conduct ranges from being spied on while dressing or showering to physical assault.
- Thirteen percent of the girls reported being forced by fellow students, teachers or other school employees to engage in sexual conduct beyond kissing.
- Just 7 percent of the victims told the school about sexual harassment. And while one in five victims told a family member, 23 percent kept quiet. More than half didn't even know if their school had a policy on sexual harassment.
- Thirty-nine percent of the victimized girls said they were afraid in school; 8 percent of the boys said they were.
- Overall, 53 percent of the students in the study said they'd been touched, grabbed or pinched in a sexual way.

munication. The challenge to parents, school personnel and community leaders is clear: We must not allow anything to threaten equity in education for all children if we are to compete effectively in the global marketplace of the next century. It is not sufficient to balance the opportunities and equalize the workforce for adult women. From the earliest ages, we must encourage a belief in equity for all children, including girls, and prevent them from encountering the barriers that allow them to doubt their own capabilities.

WHAT YOU CAN DO

Gender-Fair Teaching

- Examine your attitudes carefully. Do you believe females are generally not as skilled in math and science, and do you play that out in your interactions? Do you allow male students to control the dialogue? Do you interact with male students more than with female students? Do you discourage autonomous behavior and risk-taking in girls?
- Restrain students who dominate class discussions by not allowing interruptions, limiting the time a person may hold the floor or limiting the number of times a person may speak.
- Coach those who speak hesitantly and with too many qualifications by videotaping their participation, letting them rework their wording and then practice a more assertive delivery.
- Watch your vocabulary. Children do not necessarily translate the word "man" to mean both "man" and "woman." Nonsexist language is critical to any change in gender teaching.
- Allow girls to express their feelings, including anger. Adolescent girls become resentful if their anger is silenced, and can become defiant for this reason.

DID YOU KNOW?

Types of Harassment

These behaviors may be considered sexual harassment:

- Sexual comments, jokes, gestures or looks
- Exposure to sexual pictures, photographs, illustrations, messages or notes
- Sexual messages/graffiti
- Sexual rumors
- Implication that someone is gay or lesbian
- Spying as someone dresses or showers at school
- Flashing or mooning
- Touching, grabbing or pinching in a sexual way
- Pulling at clothing in a sexual way
- Intentionally brushing up against someone in a sexual way
- Blocking the way or cornering someone in a sexual way
- Forcing to kiss
- Forcing to do something sexual other than kiss

- Really listen to the girls. Encourage them to talk and to express their feelings.
- Discourage the image of the "perfect girl" who must become the perfect woman who never expresses anything other than good feelings for everyone.
- Discourage gender stereotyping by not scheduling male-and female-preferred courses in the same time slots during the day.

- Raise the level of awareness among school boards, school councils, superintendents and professors in schools of the positive results of equity training for teachers, counselors and administrators. Provide them copies of the AAUW report on gender teaching. Encourage release time, sabbaticals and funding for teachers to attend seminars and workshops or to take graduate courses in gender-fair education.
- Conduct research within your own school on teacher/student interaction. Provide teachers with assessment tools to check their own behavior in their classrooms.
- Develop a list of local women with expertise in educational issues for your elected officials to consider as appointees to boards of directors and education posts. Encourage women candidates who are supportive of gender-fair teaching to run for positions that influence educational policy.
- Review the books available in school and local libraries. Make sure that children and parents have access to gender-fair, multicultural materials. Provide up-to-date lists of appropriate books and materials to the librarians on a regular basis.

Curriculum

- Review in terms of gender fairness curricula and textbooks used throughout your school district. When you report your findings to the committee or board responsible for textbook and curriculum adoption, be prepared to make recommendations for change.
- Stress the necessity for a gender-fair curriculum that is fully integrated at your school, not an add-on.

- Find ways to teach mathematics equally to young children through play, using situations that introduce girls and boys early to a variety of career options. Especially show girls that math and science can have relevance in their lives.

- Inform all students about the work of outstanding women mathematicians.

- Use hands-on activities, visual representations and physical materials to demonstrate abstract concepts.

- Use group problem solving and collective brainstorming as part of your daily classroom agenda.

- Create a mathematics environment that includes and supports student examination of real life situations, such as those found in the media, concerns about social issues and so on.

- House the computer center away from the mathematics department.

- Have a wide variety of software available, including graphics, writing and art programs. Limit game playing, which attracts boys and tends to exclude girls.

- When you see a girl enjoying something on a computer, invite her to bring her friends to try it next time. Allow them to work in pairs or in groups. Set up the computer lab so that there can be eye and voice contact even if each is working on her own computer.

- Ask older girls to introduce the use of the computer to students in the lower grades.

- In history classes, have students consider what women were doing during the time period they are studying. Sometimes women were doing much the same thing as men, as evidenced by their roles in the organization of trade unions in the late nineteenth century. Or they may have done something completely different, as during World War II when women entered the workforce in great numbers, many for the first time.

- In literature, focus part of the time on women writers of the past and present who actively influenced their contemporaries and descendants.

- Women artists have practiced throughout history. Include them in chronological and stylistic surveys. Discuss the importance of women's traditional creative expressions such as needlework and quilting. Apply the same approach in the performing arts: Study the effects of women in music, theater and dance, and the institutional constraints on their becoming "great" artists.

Sexual Harassment

- Encourage the school board or local school council to provide awareness training on sexual harassment for teachers, counselors, administrators and students.

- Help your school demonstrate its strong commitment by developing and enforcing a clear policy on sexual harassment. Make sure the policy
  - explains what sexual harassment is;
  - gives some examples of unacceptable conduct;
  - clearly describes the grievance procedures and other avenues for recourse;
  - specifies what disciplinary action will be taken; and
  - is publicly posted and publicized widely.

- Make sure all students and staff know how to detect harassment, and know how to report it.

- Identify and train a few people in the school who can function as complaint managers—people who are authorized to receive confidential complaints and begin the process of dealing with them in a sensitive manner.

HOW DO YOU RATE?

Checklist on Gender Equity

YES   NO

☐ ☐   Do I generally ask boys to do heavy work in the classroom?

☐ ☐   Do I generally ask girls to do light work and secretarial chores?

☐ ☐   Do I feel sorry for girls who are unable or are unwilling to be fashionable?

☐ ☐   Do I pity boys who are unable or are unwilling to be athletic?

☐ ☐   Do I react negatively to boys who have long hair?

☐ ☐   Do I stereotype women as housewives, mothers or workers in menial or supportive positions?

☐ ☐   Do I feel that it is more important to help boys sort out career options than to help girls?

☐ ☐   Do I tend to discipline girls verbally and leniently?

(continued)

YES	NO	
☐	☐	Do I tend to discipline boys more harshly?
☐	☐	Do I encourage boys to be chivalrous?
☐	☐	Do I reward girls and boys for different things?
☐	☐	Do I display affection and displeasure in the same way toward boys and girls?
☐	☐	Do I group students according to sex in lines, on teams and so on?
☐	☐	Do I expect boys to be loud and rough and girls to be more quiet and gentle?
☐	☐	Do girls receive as much informal feedback, encouragement or praise as boys for their academic efforts?
☐	☐	Are girls interrupted more often than boys during class discussion?
☐	☐	Do boys receive more eye contact when a question is asked of the class as a whole, thus "recognizing" them and inviting responses from them?
☐	☐	Do I expect a difference in academic preference between boys and girls, with boys favoring math and science and girls preferring reading and art?
☐	☐	Do I give boys more instructions, wait time for answers or guidance time?

(continued)

YES NO

☐ ☐   Do I involve fathers as much as mothers in my communication with the students' homes?

☐ ☐   Do I schedule parent-teacher conferences when fathers are available?

☐ ☐   Do I accept and encourage an equal display of anger and pain in boys and girls?

FOR YOUR INFORMATION

Equity in Technology

Here are some available materials that address the issue of inequitable computer use in schools:

"Gender Equity in Computer Learning Environments"
Marcia C. Lynn
Computers and the Social Sciences 1 (1), pp. 19–27.
Also available through
ERIC number EJ 410 587

The Neuter Computer: Computers for Boys and Girls
Jo S. Sanders and Antonia Stone
Neal Schuman Publishers
1986
ISBN 1-555-7006-3

Off & Running: The Computer Offline Activities Book
Tim Erickson
Illustrated by Michael Allaire and William S. Wells

Equal Publishing
University of California-Berkeley, Lawrence Hall of Science
1986
ISBN 0-912-51107-9

Yes, I Can: Action Projects to Resolve Equity Issues in Educational Computing
Alice Friedman, editor
ERIC number ED 323 995

FOR YOUR INFORMATION

Math Anxiety

For girls who exhibit math anxiety in your classroom or at home, this book might help:

A Mindset for Math—Techniques for Identifying and Working with Math Anxious Girls
Published by
The Ohio State University, Columbus, Ohio.
Printed and distributed by
WEEA Publishing Center
Education Development Center, Inc.
55 Chapel Street
Newton, MA 02160

PROGRAMS THAT WORK

These individuals and groups offer training in gender-fair teaching:

Equals

Provides educator training seminars on encouraging participation and achievement of women and minority students in mathematics.

For more information, contact:

Equals
Lawrence Hall of Science
University of California-Berkeley
Berkeley, CA 94720
415-642-1823 phone

Equity Assistance Centers

There are ten federally funded centers nationwide that offer gender equity workshops.

To locate your regional center, contact:

Gender Equity Program
Mid-Atlantic Equity Center
American University
Washington, DC 20016
202-885-8536 phone

(continued)

Gesa
(Gender/Ethnic Expectations and Student Achievement)

Provides training, peer evaluation and observation of classroom dynamics.

For more information, contact:

GrayMill Consulting
2029 352nd Place
Earlham, IA 50072
515-834-2431 phone

National Women's History Project

Available for one-, two- or three-day in-service trainings on strategies and resources for integrating women's lives and accomplishments into all areas of the K–12 curriculum.

For more information, contact:

National Women's History Project
7738 Bell Road
Windsor, CA 95492
707-838-6000 phone

David Sadker

Provides workshops on correcting gender inequity for educators and community and business groups.
For more information, contact:

(continued)

David Sadker
School of Education
American University
Washington, DC 20016
202-885-3728 phone

Seed
(Seeking Educational Equity and Diversity)

Provides funds on a matching-grant basis to local school districts for training teachers to conduct ongoing faculty reading groups related to gender and multicultural equity.

For more information, contact:

National SEED Project
Center for Research on Women
Wellesley, MA 02181
617-431-1453 phone

FOR YOUR INFORMATION

Gender Teaching Resources

These are two seminal references on gender teaching and gender bias in schools:

Failing at Fairness: How America's Schools Cheat Girls
Myra and David Sadker
Charles Scribner's Sons
1994
ISBN 0-684-19541-0

How Schools Shortchange Girls
The AAUW Report
American Association of University Women
1992
ISBN 0-810-62501-6

HOW DO YOU RATE?

Checklist on Sexual Harassment in Schools

YES   NO

☐ ☐ Do you have a policy against sexual harassment?

☐ ☐ Has the policy been disseminated to staff, students and other employees?

☐ ☐ Is the information on the grievance procedure clear?

☐ ☐ Is there any reference to sexual harassment in the student discipline code?

☐ ☐ In the employee code of conduct?

☐ ☐ Do union contracts and affirmative action plans for the district contain policy language regarding sexual harassment?

☐ ☐ Are student placement work sites notified of the school's sexual harassment policy?

☐ ☐ Has there been a training program for district administration, guidance counselors and other employees, including work site supervisors?

☐ ☐ Has there been a training program for students and their parents?

PROGRAMS THAT WORK

Sample School Policy on Sexual Harassment

I. THE POLICY

    A. It is the policy of the _____ Public Schools to maintain a learning and working environment that is free from sexual harassment.

    B. It shall be a violation of this policy for any member of the _____ Public Schools staff to harass another staff member or student through conduct or communications of a sexual nature as defined in Section II. It shall also be a violation of this policy for students to harass other students through conduct or communications of a sexual nature as defined in Section II.

II. DEFINITION

    A. Sexual harassment shall consist of unwelcomed sexual advances, requests for sexual favors and other inappropriate verbal or physical conduct of a sexual nature when made by any member of the school staff to a student, when made by any member of the school staff to another staff member or when made by any student to another student when:

        1. Submission to such conduct is made either explicitly or implicitly a term or condition of an individual's employment or education, or when:

        2. Submission to or rejection of such conduct by an individual is used as the basis for academic or employment decisions affecting that individual, or when:

(continued)

3. Such conduct has the purpose or effect of substantially interfering with an individual's academic or professional performance or creating an intimidating, hostile or offensive employment or education environment.

B. Sexual harassment, as set forth in Section II-A, may include, but is not limited to the following:

1. Verbal harassment or abuse
2. Pressure for sexual activity
3. Repeated remarks to a person, with sexual or demeaning implications
4. Unwelcomed touching
5. Suggesting or demanding sexual involvement accompanied by implied or explicit threats concerning one's grades, job, etc.

III. PROCEDURE

A. Any person who alleges sexual harassment by any staff member or student in the school district may use the procedure detailed in the Fair Treatment Policy or may complain directly to his or her immediate supervisor, building principal or district ombudsman. Other building managers for informal complaints may be designated at the annual sexual harassment prevention meeting held for students and staff. Filing of a grievance or otherwise reporting sexual harassment will not reflect upon the individual's status nor will it affect future employment, grades or work assignments.

(continued)

    B. The right to confidentiality, both of the complainant and of the accused, will be respected consistent with the school district's legal obligations, and with the necessity to investigate allegations of misconduct and to take corrective action when this conduct has occurred.

IV. SANCTIONS

    A. A substantiated charge against a staff member in the school district shall subject such staff member to disciplinary action, including discharge.

    B. A substantiated charge against a student in the school district shall subject that student to student disciplinary action including suspension or expulsion, consistent with the student discipline code.

V. NOTIFICATION

Notice of this policy will be circulated to all schools and departments of the _____ Public Schools on an annual basis and incorporated in teacher and student handbooks. It will also be distributed to all organizations in the community having cooperative agreements with the public schools. Failure to comply with this policy may result in termination of the cooperative agreement. Training sessions on this policy and the prevention of sexual harassment shall be held for teachers and students in all schools on an annual basis.

(Source: Ann Arbor Public Schools, the University of Michigan, EEOC and MDE. Reprinted with permission.)

FOR YOUR INFORMATION

Resources on Sexual Harassment

The U.S. Equal Employment Opportunity Commission (EEOC) has these resources available on sexual harassment:

"Facts About Sexual Harassment"
   A two-page overview which briefly defines sexual harassment and gives examples of the circumstances under which it can occur. Tells how to file a charge with the EEOC.

"Guidelines on Discrimination Because of Sex"
Located in Title 29 of the Code of Federal Regulations at part 1604.11, this deals specifically with sexual harassment.

"Policy Guidance on Current Issues of Sexual Harassment"
EEOC Notice N-915-050
3/19/90
Provides guidance on defining sexual harassment and establishing employer liability in light of recent cases.

"Questions and Answers About Sexual Harassment"
An informative two-page leaflet giving EEOC's answers to the most commonly asked questions about sexual harassment.

For more information, contact:

U.S. Equal Employment Opportunity Commission
EEOC
1801 L Street N.W.
Washington, DC 20507
phone: 1-800-669-EEOC
1-800-800-3302 (TDD)

CHAPTER FIVE

Parents and Teachers as Partners

Most educators will agree that the difference between a good school and a great school is the degree to which parents are involved. Some of the benefits to children whose parents are active in their schools are well documented: better attendance, reduced drop-out rates and improved school achievement in general. More importantly, when parents become involved in their children's education, they themselves become more active in their communities, and even the children's teachers become more proficient, creative and motivated in regard to their work.

Of course, many schools that welcome parents' participation ask them only to lend a helping hand and to stay out of academic decisions concerning administration, curriculum and instruction. The roles of such parents are limited to those of field trip chaperones, fund-raisers for computers or band uniforms, or people who rubber-stamp decisions already made by the school or district. For years, parents have accepted these fairly insignificant roles unquestioningly.

But the true impact of the family's role in the education of their children is just now being recognized. Researchers and administrators are now saying that sharing power with parents and giving them a real voice in schools gives children more than just a boost in their academic well-being. Parental involvement is now seen as a key factor in issues ranging from building substantial school-to-community relationships, to successful integration of a multicultural perspective, to curbing school violence.

BARRIERS TO PARENT PARTICIPATION

Why, then, does the level of parental involvement in the public schools remain very low?

- Regardless of recent research attesting to the benefits, parent involvement remains a low priority for corporations that employ parents, social service agencies that are struggling to meet survival demands, and even the federal government: The U.S. Department of Education has no office with a primary mission of ensuring that parents are included in their children's education.
- Many teachers do not know how to maintain their authority and role as experts while still involving parents, and are therefore reluctant to collaborate with them. Still others simply don't know how to involve parents.
- Parents themselves have to be helped to understand what is needed. The field of education has changed tremendously in the past decade, school reforms are under way throughout the country, and new information on public education is proliferating. Unlike teachers and administrators, who have unions and other professional organizations to help keep them up-to-date on current education issues, parents get very little support in that regard, leaving them to fend for themselves.
- Parents from low income or language minority groups often have cultural perspectives and expectations that impede, or

even preclude, collaboration with the school. Some of these parents have themselves as youngsters had bad experiences with schools and feel intimidated when confronted with bureaucratic systems that they don't understand and that they feel don't value their diversity. The situation is exacerbated by some parents' inability to communicate with the school due to low proficiency in English, long working hours and time constraints, transportation difficulties, child care needs and other economic and emotional issues.

- Unless they have had training to help them work with low income and language minority parents, teachers may misread their reserved, nonconfrontational manner and noninvolvement to mean that they don't care about the education of their children. However, these parents have the same hopes and dreams for their children as everyone else. Both high and low socioeconomic status parents from all cultures have high aspirations for their children. Many simply do not know how to navigate the system, or are culturally disinclined to do so.

- Further barriers are erected with language minority parents if the materials distributed to them are written only in English. Because most school-based programs for communicating with families have been designed to accommodate the needs of middle- and upper-class mainstream families, this oversight limits the opportunities for non-mainstream families to be involved in their children's education. Families from culturally and linguistically diverse backgrounds already constitute a majority in many of our urban school districts, and their population is growing exponentially. Not offering parent materials in more than one language effectively eliminates more than one-third of our potential parent partners.

DID YOU KNOW?

What Do We Know About Parent Involvement?

Studies on parent involvement have determined many important points:

- The family provides the primary educational environment for children.
- Involving parents in their children's education improves student achievement.
- Parent involvement is most effective when it is comprehensive, long lasting and well planned.
- The benefits are not confined to early childhood or the elementary level. There are strong effects from involving parents continuously throughout high school.
- Involving parents in their children's education at home is not enough. To ensure the quality of schools as institutions serving the community, parents must be involved at all levels in the school.
- Children from low income and minority families have the most to gain when schools involve parents. Parents do *not* have to be well educated to help.
- We cannot look at the school and the home in isolation from one another. We must see how they interconnect with each other and with the world at large.

(Source: *The Evidence Continues to Grow,* A. Henderson, National Committee for Citizens in Education, Washington, DC, 1987.)

REDEFINING THE CONCEPT

Parent involvement in the nineties is badly in need of redefinition if we are to move into the next century with significantly improved chances for all of our children. Both sides of the equation—"parent" and "involvement"—need serious reengineering.

The Changing Family

As the students in our classrooms become more diverse in terms of their cultures, languages, living styles and socioeconomic status, educators will have to put aside their outdated views of the American family. When asked to describe the all-American family, most people still refer to an intact unit consisting of two children (a boy and a girl), a mother who either stays home or works only part-time and a gainfully employed father, all living together in a single family dwelling in a middle-class neighborhood. This profile describes fewer and fewer American families:

> **STRAIGHT TALK**
>
> "The closer the parent is to the education of the child, the greater the impact on child development and educational achievement."
>
> M. FULLAN, The Meaning of Change, OISE Press, Toronto, Canada

- Only 7 percent of mothers in two-parent homes stay home with the children while the father goes to work, and this number is decreasing.
- Today's households are also headed by single parents, co-

habiting parents, gay parents and families headed by relatives other than parents.

- Blended families, another common type of family unit, look very much like what most people consider a "regular" family, but the resemblance ends there. In a blended family, divorced parents with children remarry and combine their households. Instead of a common history there are two histories, along with two sets of expectations and two structures.

- Fiscal capability is also important in understanding the changing family scene. Research indicates that by the turn of the century, fully one-third of all families with children will be living in poverty.

- Another outdated myth is that of the isolated majority white family. In the near future, white children in middle-class neighborhoods are more likely than not to have African American, Hispanic and Asian children as neighborhood playmates.

- It is not uncommon for children to live in several different types of families before becoming adults.

It's time to find ways of working collaboratively with what is, in fact, our new national majority: diverse family systems.

The Concept of Involvement

Given the changing family structure, and the increasing demands on families' time and energy outside of school, it is no wonder that schools have not improved their parent involvement. Educators must recognize that there is a continuum of support levels. At the least involved, yet still valuable, level are those parents who don't come to the school but do respond to information they receive from the school about their children's education. Unfortunately, many schools don't even meet the parents' needs at this level. All parents, even those from low income and language minority families, need to know what and how their children are being taught, what the homework policies are, who to contact if they want to speak to someone about their children, what the grading procedure is, and other basic information about the school.

At the next level, parents begin to serve as helpers, supporting their children and the school by making sure their children have a quiet place to study; reinforcing good study habits at home; talking to their children about their school day; reading each day to the younger children and communicating more regularly with the teachers.

At the third level, parents become regular participants at school functions such as concerts, sports events and open houses. At this level, they also come to school to assist the teacher or staff. Children begin to feel more motivated to achieve when their parents show interest in the school simply by showing up, and their presence in the school can give teachers additional opportunities to talk with them about their children in informal ways.

At the fourth level, parents become politically active in the school. They affect the operation and program of the school itself by sharing power with the administration and making substantive and binding decisions about school operations and programs, ranging from selection of texts and materials to hiring and firing the principal.

It is important to realize that parents usually feel more comfortable progressing through the continuum rather than jumping, or being pulled, from one of the early levels to political action. It is also critical to affirm parents at whatever level they choose to operate.

The success of any parent involvement effort depends on how well it matches the needs and interests of individual families. Knowing who the parents are, including what their needs and capabilities might be, is a necessary first step in increasing their level of involvement in the school. Establishing a personal rapport between parents and someone from the school, having as many options for involvement as possible and not *requiring* high levels of commitment and participation, either explicitly or implicitly, are all very effective means of getting parents to become interested in supporting the work of the school.

More than forty million parents have children in schools in America. Real school improvement—including top-notch education for all children—will not take place without effective involvement of at least a high percentage of that group. As parents, we are the owners of the public school system and bear a responsibility to participate in it. As educators, we will be fighting an uphill battle without the participation of parents. And as citizens and consumers, we need to understand the importance of parent involvement and support parent-school partnerships as though the future of our communities depends on it, because it does.

WHAT YOU CAN DO

Parents

- The schools are yours—your taxes pay the bills. Go to school when you have an opportunity and get to know your children's teachers. Observe what happens in the classroom. Talk with the teacher, counselor, administrators and your children to learn about their needs.

DID YOU KNOW?

Types of Parent Involvement Programs

PTA meetings and bake sales are not the only ways to get parents involved in the school. Here are some alternatives to the traditional methods:

- Hotlines offering homework help for students and social service referrals to the parents
- Parent training workshops based on both student and parent needs
- Contracts that parents sign agreeing to work with their children on homework
- Home visits to students and their families
- Parent conferences focusing on career counseling for high school students
- District-wide parent meetings at a central location, not necessarily at a school, featuring information on topics many parents want, such as testing, violence in schools and so on.

- Set high expectations, and let the school know what you expect of them. Work in partnership with the educators to help them achieve your goals.
- As much as you can, volunteer your time to the school. If you have particular skills that you are willing to share—accounting, child development, art or administrative, for example—apply these skills to help the school. Recruit other parents and concerned citizens to help, too.
- Negotiate and establish rules about when, where and how

homework will be completed. Make sure your children have access to reference material, either at home or at the library, and that someone is available to help with specific problems. Always expect your children to finish their homework, and check their homework yourself when they are finished.

- Attend as many school concerts, open houses, student performances or sports activities as you can in which your children participate. Even if they are not involved in a particular event, go with them to watch their friends participate.

- Engage the place where you work to support the school. See about instituting flexible leave and child care policies so that the employees can support their children's learning.

- Find out what your employer is doing to support your local school system. Encourage them to set up school/business partnerships, opportunities for work/study programs and other initiatives.

- Become politically active in your children's school and/or district leadership through parent councils or committees under the auspices of the school administration, by attending school board meetings and so on. Encourage others to do the same.

- Work through your state and federal elected officials to ensure adequate financing for education. Since the strength and vitality of your community depends a great deal on the quality of your schools, these officials should have a vested interest in supporting your requests.

- No matter whether you have children in school, become a child's mentor. This will be enormously helpful to those children who lack role models or attentive adults in their lives. As a mentor, you can provide advice, encouragement, information, support and an example of someone who supports education.

■ Research what other communities have done to help their schools. Some of these ideas might work for your school.

FOR YOUR INFORMATION

Help for Parents

These organizations offer information and assistance to parents who want to become more involved in their children's schools:

Alliance for Parental Involvement in Education
P.O. Box 59
East Chatham, NY 12060
518-392-6900 phone

The mission of this organization is to nurture parents' natural teaching abilities and to offer them tools and resources to assist them in being active participants in the education of their children.

Parents as Teachers National Center, Inc.
9374 Olive Boulevard
St. Louis, MO 63132
314-432-4330 phone
314-432-8963 fax

This group provides information about the program Parents as Teachers (PAT), plus training and technical assistance for those interested in adopting the program, as well as information about child development, learning, constructive play and effective discipline.

Teachers

- Take a good look at how your school does or does not welcome parents into the education process.
- Let parents know that they are significant educators of their children. Give them a sense of their importance in the education of their children.
- Set up a special lounge/resource room in the school for use by parents. It need not be elaborate, but could have access to coffee, comfortable chairs or sofas, a lending library of parent aids and a display of social service agency brochures.
- To help parents assist their children at home with their academic habits, create a handbook of simple guidelines. It could contain tips and techniques dealing with formats for reports, study hints, symptoms of test or math anxiety, checklists for editing homework, information about stages of growth in child development and so on. You might want to make monthly additions to the guidebook that parents can collect in a notebook. With just a little extra work, the same material could be updated and used year after year.
- Suggest to parents that they keep dialogue journals—booklets that pass back and forth between you and the parents. Their first entry could be notes jotted down about their child's likes, dislikes, habits or anything related to their child that they feel would be important. The child carries the journal to you; you respond accordingly and send it back to the parents. Or you can initiate dialogue with parents by sending the first entry. These make wonderful com-

munication tools especially during the weeks when everyone is too busy to make face-to-face appointments.

- Many parents are truly concerned and interested in their children's education, but may have survival problems, such as earning a sufficient income to support a family, that must be addressed first. If you are aware of specifics of these difficulties, work with the school counselor in assisting the family to get the resources they need.

- Let parents know that they are wanted and needed, and don't hesitate to ask for hands-on help from them. They may be more willing to lend a hand if you are specific about the help you need, and you tell them the reasons that you need it.

- All families have strengths. Successful parent involvement programs recognize them and let the parents know that their strengths are valued.

- Cultural differences are both valid and valuable. Learn about the cultures of your students' families. Then find ways of building that information into your classroom environment.

- When working with language minority students, parent involvement becomes more relevant when it includes the extended families and the communities to which the children belong. Tap into this rich resource—aunts, uncles, grandparents, cousins and so on. Don't overlook any adult in the child's circle when thinking about "family."

- All individuals and families benefit from feeling empowered, especially at-risk families who often feel powerless and out of control.

- Successful parent involvement programs follow one basic rule: They make it easy for parents to be involved. If possible, offer services such as translation, baby-sitting and transportation to facilitate the attendance of parents at school-related meetings and activities. Distribute materials in the language of your student population. Have the meetings in places other than the school. Vary the times of the meetings and events so that all parents can come at least some of the time. Do not charge fees.

- The most difficult part of building a partnership with families is getting them to the first meeting. Impersonal efforts are largely fruitless. The best approach is as close to one-on-one as you can make it. Direct conversations with the parents in their primary language, either in person or on the phone, personalize the invitation. Direct communication will also help you understand the extent to which they might need help in order to attend the meeting.

- To retain their involvement, every meeting should respond to a specific need or concern of parents, not just address the school's general agenda.

- Make sure you are totally committed to the idea of parents being a part of your school and classroom, or don't get involved. Halfhearted attempts are worse than not trying at all.

- Don't give up if the initial response is not monumental. Many parents had bad experiences when they were students, and it takes time for them to overcome their discomfort at being so directly involved in their children's education.

HOW DO YOU RATE?

Checklist for Good Family/School Relationships

YES NO

☐ ☐ Do office personnel greet parents in a kind, friendly and courteous way, whether in person or on the phone?

☐ ☐ Do the signs at the entrance of the school welcome parents in a warm way?

☐ ☐ Are there easily followed directions for parents to find their way around the school?

☐ ☐ Is there a comfortable area for parents to wait for meetings, with a place to hang their coats and access to coffee and reading material?

☐ ☐ Are parents of students who transfer into the school at times other than the beginning of the semester given a welcoming tour and orientation to the school?

☐ ☐ Does the school permit parents to sit in on classes and observe?

☐ ☐ Do parents know where to go with their concerns and complaints?

☐ ☐ Are there clear and established procedures for dealing with parents' requests and demands?

(continued)

YES NO

☐ ☐ Are parents informed of their rights, such as access to school records, due process in disciplinary actions and participation in special education decisions?

☐ ☐ Does the school offer regular in-service training opportunities to help teachers involve and communicate with parents?

☐ ☐ Does the school stagger the times of events so that all parents can attend at least some of them?

☐ ☐ If there is a minority language population represented in the school, are written communications provided in their language?

PROGRAMS THAT WORK

Administrators might consider these common elements identified by the Southwest Educational Development Laboratory in a study of successful parent involvement programs:

- A written policy that legitimizes the importance of parent involvement
- Administrative support represented by allocation of dollars, space and people power
- Training focused on communication and partnering skills for parents and staff members

(continued)

- Emphasis on a partnership philosophy that creates a feeling of mutual ownership in the education of students
- A two-way communication structure that occurs regularly and consistently
- Networking that facilitates the sharing of information, resources and technical expertise
- Regular evaluation activity that works toward modifying program components as needed

Kentucky's School-Based Decision-Making Councils

As a result of Kentucky's landmark school reform act and its successful implementation on many levels, school-based decision-making councils have given parents, teachers and principals at each Kentucky public school substantial control over how that school operates. Each school council, advised by the school's staff, makes policies on budget allocations, curriculum, hiring and firing decisions, instructional materials and practices, schedules for the school's staff and students, uses of school space, discipline and classroom management, and extracurricular programs.

For more information about this effective program, here are two available publications:

(continued)

School-Based Decision Making
(A Guide for School Council Members and Others)
The Prichard Committee for Academic Excellence
P.O. Box 1658
Lexington, Kentucky 40592-1658
800-928-2111 phone
502-564-5680 fax

School-Based Decision Making Councils
Kentucky Department of Education
Publications Office
500 Mero Street
Frankfort, KY 40601
502-564-4201 phone
606 233-0760 fax

PART THREE

Home to School to Community

CHAPTER SIX

Multiculturalism and Your Community

It has been more than fifty years since Japanese American citizens were released from U.S. internment camps. Nearly forty years have passed since the Supreme Court ruled on bus desegregation. Three decades have transpired since the first Civil Rights Act was legislated, ending discrimination against blacks at the voting booth. Yet fear and hatred of others, especially those whom we perceive to be different from us, is still an active scourge. Throughout America—from crowded urban centers to sprawling suburbs to rural farming communities—people are grappling with this pervasive and crippling problem.

Despite the differences in population counts, ethnicity, racial demographics, unemployment figures or income levels, communities are all struggling to answer the same interrelated set of questions:

- How can we raise physically and emotionally healthy children if we can't stem the tide of hatred and violence in our neighborhoods and schools?
- What should we do to support families in their efforts to raise children who will become productive adults?

- How can we create an environment that will reclaim the growing number of children who are at risk?
- Whose responsibility is it?

These unresolved questions affect every member of our communities, regardless of whether they themselves have children. As children continue to grow up in this atmosphere of hatred, everyone loses.

PERSISTENCE OF SOCIAL PROBLEMS

One common, yet simplistic, view of solving these problems is based on proximity. If people from different cultures and backgrounds are placed in the vicinity of one another and made to interact, so the theory goes, bridges between people will be effectively built and cultural understanding will automatically result. But problems as entrenched as racism and cultural misunderstanding will not disappear so easily.

Some other factors that prevent a quick fix are the following:

- *Interconnections*
  When problems have persisted for as long as these have, they appear to be built into society almost as a natural part of everyday life. The prospect of making such drastic change leaves people frustrated and confused about where to start, and relinquishing responsibility for doing so becomes easier than sorting out the complex relationships.
- *Profit*
  Social problems often persist because someone is profiting from them. One group's loss can be another group's gain, and not only in monetary ways. Some changes are avoided

because they threaten to alter traditional authority structures; the continuing resistance to women in management positions is one such example. Other solutions may be rejected because they are in opposition to a group's pervading attitude that some of their members "deserve" more power or privilege than others. Any threat that challenges the status quo of the profit hierarchy will likely be rejected as nonsensical or too radical.

> **STRAIGHT TALK**
>
> "At the annual Lower East Side Jewish Festival yesterday, a Chinese woman ate a pizza slice in front of Ty Thuan Duc's Vietnamese grocery store. Beside her a Spanish-speaking family patronized a cart with two signs: 'Italian Ices' and 'Kosher by Rabbi Alper.' And after the pastrami ran out, everybody ate knishes."
>
> New York Times, *June 23, 1983*

- *Need for immediate gratification*

We often give up on social problems if the solutions are not immediately forthcoming. Our growing demand for quick cures is reflected in the funding cycles of grants—typically one or two years—awarded to address these issues. But it has taken generations to inculcate the attitudes of bias and exclusion we face today. It will take more than a couple of years to begin to show results.

HATE CRIMES AND GANGS

As the demographic patterns of our communities shift and our neighborhoods become more diverse, interactions with people different from ourselves are becoming increasingly common.

And as we read the daily newspapers, watch the evening news or even listen to the current rock and rap songs, we don't have to claim membership in a minority group to be able to track the increasing episodes of violence motivated by group prejudice, otherwise known as hate crimes.

WHAT DOES IT MEAN?

Hate Crime

A hate crime is any act or attempted act to cause physical injury, emotional suffering or property damage through intimidation, harassment, racial/ethnic slurs and bigoted epithets, vandalism, force or the threat of force, motivated all or in part by hostility to the victim's real or perceived race, ethnicity, religion or sexual orientation.

Hate crimes have a long history in the United States. Historically, hate crimes flare up during times of increased immigration and economic crisis—when people feel that their jobs, homes and lifestyles are threatened. German and Irish immigrants were systematically terrorized, for example, during the middle of the nineteenth century by those who condemned them for taking away jobs. Similar harassment was experienced by immigrants during the 1920s and by minorities in general during the recession of the late 1970s.

But the climate of hatred is especially frightening today: Some of our most violent perpetrators of hate crimes are young teenagers; extremists are given license to hate by radio and television talk show hosts who foment bitterness by giving airtime to the most vocal bigots; and in the current climate of intolerance and enmity, large-scale urban disturbances explode around the country, sparked by some political and religious leaders who encourage us to blame the poor and minorities for our social ills.

Today there is a hate group for every malcontent. The Klan

has groups spread throughout the country, from the Union of Independent Klansmen in McIntosh, Florida, to the American Knights of the KKK in Denver, Colorado, to the Invisible Empire Knights of the KKK in ten other states. Neo-Nazi groups are multiplying, too, and Skinheads abound: the National Aryan People's Party, Coeur D'Alene, Idaho; the White Power Liberation Front, Binghamton, New York; Aryan Revolutionary Front, Castro Valley, California; Chaotic Brothers, Louisville, Kentucky; Hammerskins, Elkhart, Indiana. Didn't get hired? Blame affirmative action. Savings and loan industry failing? Jews must be responsible. Too many children dropping out of school? Condemn those welfare mothers. It must be all their fault.

Gangs represent another serious community problem, no longer in the exclusive domain of the inner city. They cross economic, racial and religious lines. Members of many gangs—some of whom still count their age in single digits—live in a universe that gives no value to human life, does not hesitate to pull the trigger or plunge in the blade and seeks immediate gratification in every move because its citizens have no detectable future toward which they might strive. Gangs have assumed the social role no longer performed by families, and often give estranged youths a meaningful identity which they otherwise lack. That the number of gang members is dramatically increasing speaks volumes about the pathology of their lives. But gangs are the consequence of the situation, not the cause.

So what can we do to eliminate the growing gang and hate crime problem? Imprison the most villainous juvenile delinquents in each city? Pass new regulatory legislation that demands harsher punishment for those who defy the rules? Concentrate on stopping the supply of guns to children? Put up taller fences, lock more doors, shake down more kids?

Any of these solutions, if implemented effectively, will make short-term dents in crime and violence problems. But until we rectify the underlying conditions that breed our hatred and intolerance of one another, and build nurturing communities that focus on encouraging the different people who make up their fabric to live and work together in harmony, none of these measures will be effective in the long term. The dire circumstances of our children today is a gauge of our incapability to establish for them a supportive society and inclusive future.

UPDATE REPORT
Hate Crime Statistics Act of 1990

In an effort to address the problem of hate crimes, Congress passed the Hate Crime Statistics Act of 1990 (Public Law 101-275) on April 12, 1990. This act requires the Department of Justice to collect statistics on the incidents of hate crimes in America as part of its regular information-gathering system. The act is designed to serve several purposes:

- To provide the empirical data necessary to develop effective policies with which to fight the problem of hate-motivated violence.
- To raise the public awareness of the problem of hate crimes, and underscore the need for an official response.
- To help law enforcement officials measure trends, formulate effective responses, design prevention strategies and develop sensitivity to the particular needs of hate crimes' victims.

DID YOU KNOW?

The Difference Between Hate Crimes and Other Crimes

Hate crimes differ from other assaults in many ways. The special characteristics typical of hate crimes fall into the following categories:

- *Relationship of the victim to the perpetrator*
  Most assaults, including rape, involve two people who know each other well. The opposite is so for hate-motivated assaults, which are very likely to be "stranger" crimes.
- *Number of perpetrators*
  The majority of assaults involve two individuals: one victim and one perpetrator. Hate crime involves an average of four assailants for each victim, although instances of virtual mass assault are not unknown.
- *Uneven nature of the conflict*
  In addition to the frequently unfair dynamic of "ganging up" on the victim, hate crime perpetrators often attack much younger persons or arm themselves and attack unarmed victims.
- *Amount of physical damage inflicted*
  Hate crimes are extraordinarily violent. Victims are three times more likely than "normal" assault victims to require hospitalization.
- *Treatment of property*
  In a very large fraction of property crimes, something of

(continued)

value is taken. In hate-motivated crimes, it is more likely that something of value will be damaged or destroyed.

■ *Apparent absence of gain*
Not only is property more likely to be destroyed than taken in hate crime incidents, but other forms of gain are absent as well: No "personal" score is settled, no profit is made.

■ *Depersonalized target*
To be targeted for violence, the victim need not be a particular person, but only be perceived as belonging to a particular group.

■ *Places in which crime occurs*
Unlike other crime against persons and property, hate crime frequently takes place at churches, synagogues, mosques, cemeteries, monuments, schools, camps and in or around the victim's home.

(Adapted from Bodinger-deUriarte, Cristina with Sancho, Anthony R. *Hate Crime: Sourcebook for Schools*, Research for Better Schools, 1992.)

Identifying Hate Crimes

This list will help you determine whether particular incidents constitute hate crime. If the incident meets one or more of these criteria, it should be considered likely that it was at least partially hate-motivated:

(continued)

- The presence of symbols or words considered offensive to persons of a specific race/ethnicity, such as graffiti slurs or painted swastikas.
- Activities historically associated with threats to persons of a specific race/ethnicity (e.g., burning crosses, wearing swastikas or white sheets, or hanging effigies).
- The posting or circulation of demeaning jokes or caricatures based on negative stereotypes of a specific race/ethnicity.
- The defacing, removal or destruction of posted materials, meeting places, memorials and so on associated with specific racial/ethnic groups.
- Prior history of similar crimes against the same victim group.
- An act following holidays, events or activities relating to the victim's race/ethnicity.
- An act following recent or ongoing political or economic conflicts involving victim group.
- Recent or ongoing neighborhood problem involving victim group.
- Victim belief that the incident was motivated by bias against him/her as a member of a specific race/ethnicity.
- Community organizations, community leaders or residents of the community stating perceptions that the incident was motivated by bias against persons of a specific race/ethnicity.
- Perpetrator explanation/defense of incident involving exalting of perpetrator's own race/ethnicity and/or including statements demeaning victim group.
- No apparent motive for the incident.

(continued)

- The presence of organized hate group literature and/or posters or reference to an organized hate group.
- Documented or suspected organized hate group activity in the community.

(Adapted from Bodinger-deUriarte, Cristina with Sancho, Anthony R. *Hate Crime: Sourcebook for Schools*, Research for Better Schools, 1992.)

COMMUNITY SERVICES

The first step in addressing social problems is admitting that the problems exist. It is easy to point to our ethnic neighborhoods, or to the few diverse families living in our communities, and claim that the problems of racism, bigotry, hate crimes and gangs prevail in other cities and towns but not ours. Upon closer inspection, we find, of course, that although cultural sensitivity may be on the short list of community goals, it is not being given the required attention or resources, and in fact, race and ethnicity play a significant role in determining who gets their basic needs met.

STRAIGHT TALK

"We have learned that we cannot live alone, at peace; that our own well-being is dependent on the well-being of other nations, far away. We have learned that we must live as men, and not as ostriches, nor as dogs in the manger. We have learned to be citizens of the world, members of the human community."

FRANKLIN DELANO ROOSEVELT,
*Fourth Inaugural Address,
January 20, 1945*

One way to start addressing the problems is to take a good look at your community's available resources. They could include agencies that work with children and their families; businesses that are willing to get involved in transforming the community; state and federal programs; and parents and children themselves. And in motivating people to see that change is possible, don't overlook researching successful programs in communities similar to yours.

Community support is certainly an influential factor in the level of resilience children develop, and most communities already offer at least a basic set of services. However, such services may not be enough to meet the needs of a growing number of children, because they contain serious limitations:

STRAIGHT TALK

"That community is already in the process of dissolution where each man begins to eye his neighbor as a possible enemy, where nonconformity with the accepted creed, political as well as religious, is a mark of disaffection; where denunciation, without specification or backing, takes the place of evidence; where orthodoxy chokes freedom of dissent; where faith in the eventual supremacy of reason has become so timid that we dare not enter our convictions in the open lists, to win or lose."

LEARNED HAND,
speech to the Board of Regents,
University of the State
of New York,
October 24, 1952

- Most community services are crisis oriented, reactively addressing the immediate needs of people who are faced with problems that have already occurred, rather than working proactively with prevention strategies to reduce the need for intervention. Similarly, many services concentrate on a family's weaknesses rather than its strengths.

- Because of the growing need for community services, decreased funding and the limitations of existing staff, services are generally provided *to* families and children rather than developed in collaboration *with* them. It is far easier to make rapid, crisis decisions about what is best for children and families than to spend the considerable time and energy it takes to learn about the complexities of their problems, and what their own goals and objectives might be.

- In some cases, the services people need are simply not available. For others, even if the services are available, they are inaccessible. And there is no single agency responsible for helping families navigate their way through the maze, either. For still others, the services offered may be unacceptable, either because the services contradict their cultural values or because acceptance of the services makes the families feel that they have lost control of their lives.

- One of the most serious (yet most easily remedied) ways community service programs fall short is that they function independent of one another. Each has its own mission, sources of funding, eligibility requirements, guidelines for helping its constituents and so on. There is rarely, however, a single coordinating organization, which could easily ensure comprehensive and non-duplicative services.

If we want to create a system that corrects these flaws, we should be listening to the workers who are currently delivering the services and to the families themselves. They know, and have not been reluctant to say, what direction a new system should take and what its key characteristics would be. They want a system that is comprehensive, preventative, both family-centered

DID YOU KNOW?

Some Forms of Cross-Cultural Communication

- *Interracial communication*

  This form of communication occurs when source and receiver are from different races. Interracial communication may or may not be intercultural. The major difficulty encountered in interracial communication is an attitudinal problem associated with racial prejudice. A person who holds stereotypes about other races usually expects certain behavior or responses that might not occur.

- *Interethnic communication*

  This refers generally to situations where source and receiver are of the same race but are of different ethnic backgrounds or origins. Although they may be members of the same pervading majority North American culture (Greek Americans and French Americans, for example) and the same race, there may still be distinct differences between them.

- *International communication*

  This refers primarily to communication between nations and governments. It is the communication of diplomacy and propaganda, and it frequently involves both interethnic and interracial situations. This form of communication can be highly ritualized, taking place in neutral countries, the United Nations or between diplomatic third parties.

and family-driven, flexible, integrated and sensitive to cultural, racial and gender matters. Such an infrastructure would go a long way toward providing all children a cohesive network of support, and would allow both parents and community members to become effective partners in their children's healthy development.

COMMUNICATING ACROSS CULTURES

Shaping a new form of inclusive community interaction will take creativity, awareness, caring, knowledge and sensitivity. It will take a strong belief that the efforts will be beneficial to everyone. And it will require learning new skills to communicate across cultures.

Part of the challenge of communication is that it is culture-bound: The way we communicate is a product of our culture. Language habits—along with eating habits, social acts, economic and political activities and so on—follow patterns of culture. What people do, how they act and how they live and communicate are both a response to and a function of their culture.

Culture and communication cannot be separated. Not only does culture mandate who talks with whom about what, and dictates the form and pattern of that communication, but it also helps establish how people understand the meanings those mes-

DID YOU KNOW?

Communication

In addition to language, vocabulary and pronunciation, these are some other ways in which aspects of communication differ from group to group:

- Taking turns during conversations
- Ways in which conversations are initiated or ended
- Interrupting
- Using silence as a communicative device
- Appropriate topics
- Interjection of humor
- How much or how little to talk
- Sequencing the elements of a conversation

sages have and the conditions under which they may or may not be sent, noticed or interpreted. Culture is the foundation of communication. As self-motivated human beings living in a country where the rights of the individual are held in the highest esteem, we may feel uncomfortable about such conditioning. The fact is, nonetheless, that when cultures vary, communication practices also vary. And if we can begin to understand these differences, we can reduce or eliminate the anger, fear and unresolved emotions that they cause.

With more than a million immigrants entering our country each year, and with hundreds of cultures already represented here, it is critical that we learn to build meaningful relationships with our neighbors despite cultural and language differences. It is time to stretch our cultural comfort zone, adapt to the change that is around us and learn to benefit from the richness of our diversity, for the sake of our children and their future.

WHAT YOU CAN DO

Hate Crime and Gangs

- Encourage people to report hate crimes by posting in conspicuous areas permanent notices about how to do so.
- Establish and maintain a central depository for reports of bias-related incidents and hate crimes. Regularly publish updates to the depository to keep the awareness level of hate crime high.
- Train school counselors in techniques of victim-assistance and/or victim-referral to outside sources.
- Assist all community organizations, including religious congregations, women's groups and service clubs, to develop a plan for responding to hate crimes.
- Work with your local government to establish contingency plans to respond quickly to incidents and prevent escalation into broader community conflicts.
- In order to be prepared to respond effectively to gangs in your community, develop a balanced anti-gang "readiness" program that includes both awareness of and resistance to school violence and intimidation. Parent involvement, along with school and community commitment, is essential.
- Implement a gang-prevention program in your community that includes the following:

1. Recreational programming available to all youth in the community
2. Employment training and development
3. Peer counseling program
4. Training of service providers for at-risk youth
5. Publication of a cross-agency resource directory of services provided to at-risk youth in the community
6. Parent education

FOR YOUR INFORMATION

Hate Crime References

Here are three excellent references on hate crime to help you address the issue in your school or community:

Hate Crime: Sourcebook for Schools
by Cristina Bodinger-deUriarte
with Anthony R. Sancho
Published by
Research for Better Schools
666 N. Third St.
Philadelphia, PA 19123-6107
ISBN 1-566-02046-8
215-576-9123 phone
215-576-0133 fax

Hate Crimes: The Rising Tide of Bigotry and Bloodshed
by Jack Levin and Jack McDevitt
Published by
Plenum Press

233 Spring St.
New York, NY 10013
ISBN 0-306-44471-2
212-260-8000 phone
212-463-0742 fax

When Hate Groups Come to Town
Published by
Center for Democratic Renewal
P.O. Box 50469
Atlanta, GA 30302-0469
404-221-0025 phone
404-221-0045 fax

FOR YOUR INFORMATION

The following resource organizations can provide information and technical assistance on dealing with hate crimes:

Anti-Defamation League of B'nai B'rith

This human rights organization sponsors a variety of programs to reduce religious, racial and ethnic prejudice, and improve intergroup relations. Among their successful endeavors is the World of Difference Program, now in use throughout the country.

For more information, contact:

Anti-Defamation League of B'nai B'rith
6505 Wilshire Boulevard, Suite 814
Los Angeles, CA 90048
213-655-8205 phone

Center for Democratic Renewal

Originally founded in 1979 as the National Anti-Klan Network (NAKN), this organization was set up to monitor, collect, document, analyze and make up-to-date predictions on the changing and complex trends of hate groups. The center provides technical assistance to community-based groups who are victims of hate crimes or who need assistance in organizing an anti-racist campaign. Ask for their "Ten Points to Remember When Responding to Hate Groups" bulletin.

For more information, contact:

Center for Democratic Renewal
P.O. Box 50469
Atlanta, GA 30302-0469
404-221-0025 phone
404-221-0045 fax

Klanwatch Project

This project was started in 1980 to help curb Ku Klux Klan and racist violence through litigation, education and monitoring. Since then, lawsuits brought by SPLC and Klanwatch have resulted in a number of federal civil rights indictments.

For more information, contact:

Klanwatch Project
Southern Poverty Law Center
400 Washington Ave.
Montgomery, AL 36104
205-264-0286 phone

Communication

- Consider the relevant cultures and adapt your message accordingly, using the appropriate type of courtesy and respect for country, culture or beliefs.
- Keep your message concise, and make sure it is clear. Use logical transitions and include necessary details so your message is complete.
- Be aware of different cultural rules for attentiveness during conversations, for physical distance between speakers and for entering conversations that are already in progress.
- Remember that dialogue is more affirming than monologue. Dialogue requires a genuine involvement with the other person. To engage in a dialogue, you must be willing to compare the ideas, opinions, beliefs, feelings and attitudes of others with your own.
- Similarly, acceptance is more confirming than interpretation. When you draw inferences and reach conclusions about another person's remarks that go far beyond anything that person thought that she said, it will be difficult to resolve any differences there may be between you. When you respond to another person's statements by genuinely trying to understand his thoughts and feelings and by reflecting that understanding in your responses, you show acceptance for what the other person is saying. You need not agree with a person to be able to understand her.

PROGRAMS THAT WORK

Creative Response and City at Peace

An original musical which voices teenage concerns about racism, drug abuse and other difficult issues facing young people and their families today, *City at Peace* transforms Washington, DC, from a place torn by drugs and violence in 1993 to a harmonious community in 2010. The play, which calls for an end to stereotyping and mistrust, is based on actual experiences of the participants, and is a project ative Response, a not-for-profit organization which promotes international peace, education and cross-cultural understanding through the performing arts.

Creative Response helps local groups get started and gain sponsorship for their own *City at Peace* production. It conducts month-long programs for youth ages twelve to nineteen, who join to develop and perform the musical play, and encourages the children to tear down the traditional barriers that separate them.

For more information on *City at Peace* or how to begin a program in your community, contact:

Creative Response
800-275-7231 phone

FOR YOUR INFORMATION

Creating Community Anywhere: Finding Support and Connection in a Fragmented World
by Carolyn R. Shaffer and Kristin Anundsen
1993

This is a comprehensive reference on developing functioning communities, and will be useful whether you live in an urban, suburban or rural area. It provides detailed guidelines for building effective communities, and profiles several existing successful models around the country.
Published by:

The Putnam Publishing Group
200 Madison Avenue
New York, NY 10016
ISBN 0-87477-746-1

CHAPTER SEVEN

Actions as Antidotes: Working for Change

There is an old riddle that asks, "What's the difference between ignorance and apathy?" The lamentable answer is "I don't know and I don't care."

In fact, most of us do know the difference between being ignorant (lacking education or knowledge, from the Latin *ignorare,* meaning "not to know") and being apathetic (feeling or showing a lack of interest or concern, from the Greek *apatheia,* meaning "without feeling"). But despite our awareness that we are headed for a dismal future, and propelling our children toward an even more catastrophic scenario, we just don't seem to care about changing things. Or, more accurately, we *do* care when we first hear about the bleak details:

- Twenty percent of all of our children are growing up in poverty, a 21 percent increase since 1970.
- One in every four homeless persons in cities is a child.
- The rate of suicide among adolescents has tripled since 1960.
- Violence is approaching the position of being America's number one public health problem.

- The carnage of street gang–related murders in the United States is statistically higher than that of Belfast.
- Among youths age fifteen to nineteen, the risk of being shot to death more than doubled in the past decade.
- In addition to violence in the community, at least 3.3 million children each year are at risk of witnessing parental abuse, a conservative estimate because of underreporting of domestic abuse.

But our sympathy ebbs just as fast as it is aroused. We are overwhelmed by competing disasters and are suffering from what writer Anna Quindlen calls a "hardening of the arteries of kindness." We are burned out. We are suffering from compassion fatigue.

COMPASSION FATIGUE

The malignant and corrosive forces in our society that are threatening the future of our children are also traumatizing those of us who are their care givers, diminishing our ability to meet their needs. A 1992 Harris poll backs up this theory with a frightening statistic: 89 percent of adults live in chronic stress. When we are immobilized by this stress, and by our own despair and resistance to change, we can't do much to help our children. We compound their problems instead.

Compassion was not always such a difficult response. The world was seen as a much simpler place, with areas that we broadly described as "Asia," or "Africa," or "the Soviet Union." World disasters weren't broadcast into our homes with the same immediacy we experience today. Closer to home, the mentally ill were locked away in institutions, not set adrift to homelessly wander our streets; teen pregnancies and suicides were not openly discussed; the

> **STRAIGHT TALK**
>
> "Despite two decades of covering the very social problems that have led to compassion fatigue I haven't caught the bug. Why? Because instead of seeing the problem, I see the person."
>
> ANNA QUINDLEN

"isms"—racism, sexism, classism—were rarely spoken about as issues. There were simply fewer things to which we were called upon to be sympathetic.

Now we are exhorted on a daily basis to be "compassionate" toward the poor, the misguided, the homeless, the victims. World and neighborhood conflicts, however, are not as neat and trim as they seem when we watch them on television, sandwiched between advertisements for credit cards and fast food. Relief efforts take months or years, not the microseconds it takes the media to draw us into the disasters. They quickly become old news. We throw away the unopened fund-raising letters; skip the current updates in the paper; turn away. We literally and figuratively change the channel.

REACTIONS TO TROUBLED TIMES

In her insightful and prescriptive book *Despair and Personal Power in the Nuclear Age,* Joanna Macy cites three ways in which people respond to the slew of requests for understanding and assistance in the face of today's social problems:

Disbelief

Unless they become personalized, social problems appear as abstract concepts to most of us. If they don't affect us directly (seeing them in action in film or on television doesn't count), we find it hard to believe that they really exist. So despite the increasing frequency of violence, racism and hate crime in this country, many people refuse to take it seriously because they simply don't believe it.

Denial

Until the breakup of the Soviet Union, it was the possibility of total annihilation that we denied. Today, as our inability to accept differences among one another grows and the instances of conflict and violence hit closer to home, we do not deny the danger of our situation so much as what is at stake. As Ms. Macy says, "The human mind is tempted to acquiesce to the triviality of its own existence. It is tempted to say, 'What is so special about human beings?' "

Double Life

Repressing the knowledge of the rising tide of hatred and violence drains us of the very energy we need to fight against those phenomena. On one level, we lead our lives thinking that nothing much has changed, as we take the children to school, shop at the malls and attend the religious services of our choice. But we know on another level that *everything* has changed. And without the knowledge of how to integrate these two layers of consciousness, we live in both of them, with the vague feeling that our own neighborhoods could go at any minute.

STRAIGHT TALK

"If we do not change our direction we are likely to end up where we are headed."

Chinese proverb

I would add a fourth response to this list:

Despair

Despair is an acknowledgment of the shortcomings of human beings, the despondent awareness that the lives we dreamed about may not come to fruition, the painful realization that we cannot shape the world according to our desires simply by wishing it so. It is an overwhelming sense of futility and defeat, coupled with a loss of hope. Our real problem is not indifference; it is dread.

Whether we call it "burnout," "compassion fatigue" or "despair," it anesthetizes us, and can create a sense of isolation. Like rats in a laboratory that turn away and busy themselves in a frenzy of unrelated activity when they are introduced to a threat that they cannot remove, we develop an insatiable appetite for pleasurable diversions: We frantically consume goods and entertainment products—anything that will distract us from problems too big to contemplate.

After living for long enough with this sense of social illness, we begin to blame others for our situation, creating scapegoats on whom we can focus our anger. Our ability to be clear about our lives diminishes. At moments of heightened danger, the measures of cognitive functioning are consistently lower. Under such stressful conditions, the information we do choose to take in is not processed well. The repression of a strong emotion such as despair, it seems, greatly impairs our capacity to think and communicate.

COMMITMENT TO CHANGE

As parents, educators, community leaders and friends of children everywhere, we have a special commitment to the future. We must learn to confront our despair; to acknowledge that what we fear will not go away; to break the taboo about dealing publicly with our concerns for the future by deciding that we as individuals, families, schools and communities are willing to talk and are open to listening; and to truly believe that it is our responsibility to do so. As the awareness of our social problems increases, we are being presented with a rare window of opportunity to significantly improve the chances our children will have for a better future. Whether we look at the issues from an economic, political

STRAIGHT TALK

"Think of many things. Do one."

Portuguese saying

or social perspective, it is imperative that we recognize the need for change.

Resistance to change is both unavoidable and normal. As with all living organisms, it is our natural reaction to try and stop anything that we perceive as potentially harmful. When we oppose change, we are struggling to remain inside our comfort zones—those areas beyond whose boundaries lie confusion and chaos—in order to maintain consistency and balance in our lives.

One way of becoming comfortable with change, and to successfully implement change in our homes, schools and communities, is to understand some of its various dimensions:

> **STRAIGHT TALK**
>
> "You can't mandate what matters.
>
> "You can mandate new taxes, new textbooks, new things that should be done or must be done. But the heart of change—the skills and the know-how, the commitment and the motivation, the attitudes—cannot be mandated, cannot be mobilized from the top."
>
> MICHAEL G. FULLAN, Change: A Guide for the Perplexed

- If people are to commit themselves to innovation, risking the inevitable anxieties and discomfort that accompany it, they must find the mission and the new objectives preferable to what they are currently experiencing, and achievable as well.
- People who possess the readiness for change—who are flexible, energetic and invested in it—will progress through its stages much more easily than those who don't. People who are more rigidly invested in their personal concerns, such

as maintenance of power and position, are more sensitive to the stresses of change, leaving them to be less willing participants.

- Two of the greatest needs during change are technical support—training and materials—and clear communication. It is a dictum of organizational change that the larger the innovation the greater the need for communication. Remembering that change usually begets confusion and misunderstanding, and that that commotion, if unchecked, will spell failure, will help assure clarity throughout the process.

- During the early stages of change, when uncertainty is the highest, offering those who are involved even modest amounts of reassurance and recognition is a strategy repeatedly endorsed in studies of change.

Where Do We Begin?

In their book *War and Anti-War*, Alvin and Heidi Toffler assert that creating harmonious communities cannot depend on first solving all of our social, moral and economic problems. The issue is not how to build consensus in a perfect world but how to build it in the one in which we are actively living and creating. We can't wait for governmental grants to appear, for everyone on our block to join up or for our leaders to give us the go-ahead. All of us need to believe that we can make change happen, to join our efforts with other like-minded individuals and, at the very

STRAIGHT TALK

"Never doubt that a small group of thoughtful, committed people can change the world. Indeed, it's the only thing that ever has."

MARGARET MEAD

DID YOU KNOW?

Anyone interested in creating change needs to locate the sources of resistance against their efforts. Some sources are as follows:

- Disagreement with the values underlying a change
- Confusion over the meaning and importance of a change
- Lack of a political or other power base to make change
- Lack of personal courage to risk a fight
- Lack of a clear structure to use for changes
- Lack of skill in knowing how to innovate
- Lack of knowledge of program options
- Lack of knowledge of the true dimensions of the problems and issues
- Champion of the change is not credible
- Insufficient dissatisfaction with the status quo
- Tenacious wish to abide by tradition
- Lack of sufficient commitment to the goals of the change

least, to say no to anything we feel is going in the wrong direction.

There is a story about a man who was watching an old woman walk along an ocean beach. She had a strange pattern to her stride—every few steps she would stop, bend down, throw something in the water and then walk along some more. When he came closer the man saw that the old woman was picking up live starfish that had washed up on shore during the previous night's storm, and throwing them back into the ocean one at a time. He was appalled at the lunacy of her effort.

"Do you realize how fruitless a task this is?" he asked. "There are literally thousands of starfish along the shore. You can't possibly make a difference. You might as well stop right now and relax."

She listened politely to what he said, bent down, picked up another starfish and gazed at it thoughtfully for a moment.

"It makes a difference to this one," she replied as she threw it back into the ocean.

It is crucial to the future of our children that we comprehend and trust this simple fact: Individuals *can* make a difference—all the difference in the world. It will only be through the persistent effort of each of us that changes will be made that allow our children to live, learn and work together to achieve common goals in a culturally diverse world. Without change and immediate intervention, our children will continue the same cycles of conflict and hatred that they are experiencing today.

STRAIGHT TALK

"If there is anything that we wish to change in the child, we should first examine it and see whether it is not something that could better be changed in ourselves."

CARL GUSTAV JUNG

WHAT YOU CAN DO

- Decide that you will help; but understand first, act later.
- Consider your comfort. Is there one issue or another you feel comfortable addressing? Which strategies do you prefer?

- Understand that things happen for a reason, that we live in a cause-and-effect world and that we can change the way things turn out if we influence the causes. This is called "empowerment," and it is one of the most important concepts to comprehend when trying to make changes happen around us. We can be most effective when we feel that we have some control over our lives.

- Recognize that the enormity of the problems has advantages: Everyone has an opportunity to help find solutions and each of us can make a big difference.

- Begin with one thing that needs attention. Perhaps you have read something in this book that has sparked your interest. There might be an issue in your community or school that concerns you. It needn't be a big job or a big issue, but overcome the inertia and start somewhere.

- Get to know the issue. Learn by reading, attending meetings and lectures, watching films and videotapes and talking to others who are involved.

- Have a clear idea of what you want to accomplish. As much as possible, identify your goals and develop an action plan for achieving them. But also expect your ideas about change to evolve over time. Expect change to be turbulent at times and almost always slower than you think it will be.

- Rather than reinventing the wheel, build on what already works. Find examples of successes in other communities and schools and model your action plan after them.

- Know why you are getting involved, what prompted your effort to make changes and what your purpose is for being involved.

- Develop a base of support including others who share your ideas and dreams and those who will offer you moral support even though they themselves are not involved with your work.

- Create a teaching group by building capacity in others, exponentially expanding your efforts. Determine which skills your group members already have that they can pass along to others, and learn from one another.
- Planning your time carefully can serve as one of the best defenses against burnout. You will be calling yourself a failure when you aren't one if you plan your time unrealistically. For example, when making out your schedule, allow for lag time. Everything will take much longer than you think it's going to.
- Know the difference between flawlessness and excellence. Work need not be perfect to be effective.
- Don't play "total expert." Acknowledging what you don't know makes you more trustworthy. But do your homework so that you can be responsible for what you do say.
- Use your strengths and personal resources:
  1. Knowledge of the issues
  2. Ability to work with people
  3. Energy
  4. Support from family, friends and coworkers
  5. Ability to run a meeting, organize others, speak in public
  6. Connections to powerful people
  7. Visibility in your community
  8. Writing skills
- Don't be afraid to share personal experiences. The dangers we are dealing with are abstract and remote from many people's daily lives. The issues become more real for them when they see that they have affected real people.
- Formal and informal support from top officials is crucial. Look for the power in your community or school, because

that's usually where change is controlled, and learn how the system works. Who holds the power? Where are decisions made? How are they made? What is the relationship between those who make the decisions and those who benefit from them? Who pays to have the decisions of the power group carried out?

- Find out if those you work for and buy from support your views, so you can make conscious choices. If you own stock, attend shareholder meetings and raise issues.
- Your voice is important, so get in touch with your congressional representatives and senators. Send a letter or make a local phone call. Ask five friends to do so, too. All together, your team is equal to hundreds of people—a phone call represents the view of 50; a letter represents the view of 100; a phone call and a letter is 150; a telegram is 250.
- When you write letters, use these tips to make it easier:
  1. Keep an "action file" of current articles together in one place.
  2. Address and stamp several envelopes at one time.
  3. When you are asked to write, do it immediately.
  4. Write to your senators every week or two before each vote on the issues. Write to your representatives each month and before each vote.
  5. Keep it short and simple.

6. Do not mail preprinted letters. Use your own words and thoughts.

7. Be specific about what you want people to do.

- People are less likely to reject your views if you can show them how a new idea fits in with what they already believe, and if you have anticipated their fears and concerns in dealing with the issues. Address fears before they have a chance to surface.

- Ideas that seem silly, weird or alarming may not be viable solutions themselves, but if you can take them seriously enough to use them to start fresh trains of thought, they often lead to new and much more practical possibilities.

- Community service is not just for high school and college students and adults. We can start with the very youngest children, reinforcing their behavior through childhood and adolescence and into adulthood. Most children have a very keen sense of justice and care as much as we do about others who are hurt, and they can contribute their energy and skills through structured activities. Public service can help empower them, too, to live lives of dignity and purpose while channeling their energy toward constructive responses to diversity, change and conflict.

STRAIGHT TALK

"Beware of: Justification of procrastination. Paralysis of analysis."

MARTIN LUTHER KING, JR.

"The fight must go on. The cause of civil liberty must not be surrendered at the end of one or even one hundred defeats."

ABRAHAM LINCOLN

■ Be willing to let go of a discussion at the right time. There is a moment when it is best to leave things as they are in order to allow change to occur, and you may never know if it has occurred as a result of your discussion. To develop patience, it might help to recall those experiences when you went through a personal change and the change agent—a book, a film, a speaker, an encounter—had no idea you were affected.

■ Avoid what Joe Flower, editor of *The Change Letter*, calls the "Daddy Syndrome," in which we refer upward to what "they" think we ought to do—the government, our boss, the past. Trust your instincts. If you believe in what you are doing and you believe that what you are doing is right, you will not only draw others who share your beliefs, but you also stand a terrific chance of drawing others who are skep-

STRAIGHT TALK

"If the problem of denial is to be overcome, it is necessary to do more than merely scare people with horrendous pictures of the possible future. Indeed, the more horrendous the picture which is drawn, the more it is likely to result in denial and pathological inactivity . . . It is hard for people to visualize the nature of the system change which is necessary for survival. This then is one of the major tasks today of the political scientist, the philosopher, the journalist and the prophet: to give people an image of changes in the international system which seems small enough to be feasible yet large enough to be successful."

KENNETH E. BOULDING,
"The Prevention of World War III,"
The Virginia Quarterly Review,
Vol. 38, No. 1
(Winter 1962), pp. 1–12

tical, curious, unconvinced and/or just plain unenlightened.

- Don't wait to celebrate until the job is finished—because it rarely is. Commemorate the incremental changes, and give yourself and others credit and recognition frequently along the way.

- It takes energy to care, and physical stamina. Care for yourself with the same energy that caring for others requires. This may mean something as simple as eating properly and getting enough sleep.

- Maintain your personal focus during the course of your involvement. Being personally centered helps to provide energy for all of the facilitating, listening and mediating work that goes on. When you feel heavy resistance from a group or the community, always try to return to what is personally important and meaningful in this work for you.

- Develop and maintain hope, not optimism. Optimism is an expectation, a tendency to expect the best possible outcome. Hope on the other hand is a proactive commitment, a confidence in, and dedication to, the future. Hope takes a realistic view of the present and does what it can to bring about a positive future. Its opposite is despair.

HOW DO YOU RATE?

Are Your Community Leaders Helping or Hindering?

YES NO

☐ ☐ Do your community leaders give access to their constituents? Are they readily available for official action, questions and discussion?

☐ ☐ Do they back up your requests with formal and informal clout?

☐ ☐ Have they made it publicly clear that your program has priority and that agency resources, especially professional time, are to be devoted to it?

☐ ☐ Do they include community members in their policy meetings when discussing your issues?

☐ ☐ Do they help get community members on the agenda of major state and professional meetings?

☐ ☐ Do they come to your meetings and conferences as both speakers and participants?

☐ ☐ Do they hire and promote women and minorities to top jobs and urge others to do the same?

☐ ☐ Do they mention your program independently and supportively?

FOR YOUR INFORMATION

The Change Letter is a newsletter about change—how we identify what works and what doesn't, deal with it better, make use of it and find power in its turbulence. It addresses both personal and organizational change, applying the insights of chaos theory to practical everyday situations.

For more information, contact:

Joe Flower
The Change Project
42 Heather Way
Larkspur, CA 94939
415-924-5036 phone
415-924-0145 fax
bbear @ well.com e-mail
http://www.well.com/www/bbear/: World Wide Web site

Knowledge for Action: A Guide to Overcoming Barriers to Organizational Change
Chris Argyris
Jossey-Bass Publishers
350 Sansome Street
San Francisco, CA 94104
1993
ISBN 1-55542-519-4

Although written primarily for organizational researchers, this is a valuable book for anyone who is interested in learning more about the nature of social change and barriers to change. Argyris presents a step-by-step description of how to assess an organization's capacity to learn, analyze the data and design and implement effective interventions that help create more dynamic and innovative organizations. He includes checklists, charts and scoring procedures that can be used to make lasting changes in the status quo.

FOR YOUR INFORMATION

Here are some wonderful books that can help to empower young people. The fiction books all have children or young people as the protagonists in their fight for social justice. The nonfiction books can serve as how-to manuals for social activism.

Fiction

Steal Away . . . to Freedom
Jennifer Armstrong
Scholastic Books
New York, NY
1992
Grades 5 and up
Two girls—one black and one white—escape on the Underground Railroad and each tells her story from her own perspective.

The Island on Bird Street
Uri Orlev
Houghton Mifflin
Boston, MA

1984
Grades 5 and up
A young boy, alone in a Warsaw ghetto, draws on his own resources
to survive.

The Little Weaver of Thai-Yen Village
Khanh Tuyet Tran
Children's Book Press
Emeryville, CA
1986
Grades 3 and up
A young Vietnamese girl wounded in the war struggles to maintain her
cultural identity while adjusting to life in America.

Farewell to Manzanar
Jeanne Wakatsuki Houston and James D. Houston
Bantam Books
New York, NY
1983
Grades 6 and up
The story of a Japanese-American family's four years at Manzanar in-
ternment camp during World War II as seen through the eyes of a
child.

The Streets Are Free (La Calle es Libre)
Kurusa
Firefly Books
Scarsborough, Ontario, Canada
1981
Grades 3 and up
A group of children in a Caracas slum struggle to get a park.

Sidewalk Story
Sharon Bell Mathis
Puffin
New York, NY
1986
Grades 3 and up
A nine-year-old girl feels awful when her best friend gets evicted from her apartment, so she does something about it.

Sadako and the Thousand Paper Cranes
Eleanor Coerr
Dell
New York, NY
1977
Grades 3 and up
A true story about the strength and spirit of an eleven-year-old Japanese girl, who dies from the radiation poisoning she suffered in the bombing of Hiroshima.

A Hand Full of Stars
Rafik Schami
Puffin
New York, NY
1990
Grades 6 and up
A first-person account of a Syrian boy who becomes increasingly angry with the repressive Syrian government, which eventually arrests and tortures his father. He keeps a journal and publishes an underground newspaper.

Nonfiction

It's Our World Too: Stories of Young People Who Are Making a Difference
Phillip Hoose
Little, Brown and Co.
New York, NY
1993
Grades 6 and up
Accounts of young people who have worked on various social justice issues.

The Kid's Guide to Social Action: How to Solve the Social Problems You Choose—and Turn Creative Thinking into Positive Action
Barbara Lewis
Free Spirit Publishing
Minneapolis, MN
1991
Grades 7 and up
A useful handbook including sample formats for letters, petitions and lists of contact organizations.

A Kid's Guide to How to Stop the Violence
Ruth Harris Terrell
Avon Books
New York, NY
1992
Grades 4 and up
An easy to understand explanation of the violence that affects children, and ideas on what kids can do about them.

CHAPTER EIGHT

Our Universal Challenge

"What is faith worth if it is not translated into action?"

MOHANDAS KARAMCHAND (MAHATMA) GANDHI

"Collateral damage" is a term typically used when describing the aftermath of a battle, an all-encompassing term describing the losses incurred. In today's world, awash with violence and hatred, no one is suffering more than our children. They have become the collateral damage of the shadow side of our American character.

Sociologists speak of a lost generation. Psychiatrists talk about children who are suffering from post–traumatic stress disorder. Educators and parents see children whose defining attitude is nihilism, children who sense that it doesn't matter what they do because they won't live long enough to suffer the consequences. Watching them grow up in fearful and dehumanizing circumstances, we find it too painful to predict the individual and social repercussions of raising children who measure human worth in terms of their ability to obtain weapons or escape accountability for their actions.

Individually, every parent and educator is concerned about

his or her child's future. But when we bring together people of different races or cultures to reach agreement about how to ensure the worth of that future, denial, hostility and fear of diversity continue to destroy the chances we have to create it, as they lay the foundation for more physical and emotional killing. Multiculturalism is not the force that is threatening our unity. Rather, it is our inability to accept our differences and our unwillingness to honor the very ideals we espouse that are draining the vitality of our nation and preparing our children to hate.

Ironically, we understand and accept the need for biological and botanical diversity as a requirement for the survival of a given species. None of our oceans, forests, woods or ponds would survive without their diverse constellation of organisms, for example, and this variety is often used as a measure of their health and potential for growth and survival.

We are not so understanding and accepting of the variables of humankind—cultural, religious, national, linguistic—despite the fact that our population is already hybrid and becoming increasingly so. No race or culture holds a monopoly on prejudice and intolerance. Are you a Jew who harbors a generations-old resentment for Germans? A

STRAIGHT TALK

"The truth is, young people are not saved by bureaucrats sitting behind desks in Washington, DC, or, for that matter, Atlanta, Georgia. They're saved one at a time by people like you, by volunteers in churches and boys clubs, and by teachers and coaches in schools. And most importantly, they're saved at home. Abraham Lincoln said it simply, 'The hand that rocks the cradle rules the world.'"

JAMES O. MASON,
Assistant Secretary for Health,
Department of Health and Human
Services, and Head, Public Health
Service, 1991

white person who discounts all black people? A black person who hates or envies a biracial person? A man who is resentful of women? On the one hand, these generalizations exist because the human mind catalogs and generalizes in order to maintain balance and order. On the other hand, each of us is human and deserving of respect. It is possible to sensitize ourselves against stereotypes and prejudice. And it is crucial to the future of our children that we understand what a group of UNESCO scholars articulated in 1967: that we are

> capable of learning to share in a common life, to understand the nature of mutual service and reciprocity and to respect social obligations and contracts. Such biological differences as exist between members of different ethnic groups have no relevance to problems of social and political organization, moral life and communication between human beings. Biological studies lend support to the ethic of universal brotherhood (and sisterhood). Humankind is a social being who can reach his or her fullest potential only through interaction.

Most religious and spiritual beliefs have recognized the fundamental unity of the human family; the equality and dignity of all human beings; the belief that love, compassion and unselfishness have greater power than hate, prejudice, enmity and self-interest; and that might does not make right. We should ask ourselves to what extent we are providing role models for our children. To what extent are we providing a safe and receptive environment for them to grow in? To what extent do our words and actions promote peaceful relations among others? It is time that we come out of denial, stop avoiding the issues and begin to practice what we preach in real life and in real time:

- We must recognize the enormity of the preventable problems related to hatred, defensiveness and inhumanity, and that our willingness to find solutions is vital to our moral and economic well-being.
- The education of all of our children from its earliest beginnings must be centered on the development of their ability to think, and should deepen and extend their positive human potential. It is in the mind of each of us that the foundations for peace in our local and world communities is constructed. If we are to be peacemakers, we must each be peace thinkers and peace feelers.
- We must stop separating what is happening in Mogadishu from Manhattan, Bosnia from Birmingham, the Middle East from Minneapolis. If we think that what is occurring in our neighborhoods is any different from what is occurring in other troubled areas throughout the world where people are unable to accept one another's differences, we are wrong.
- Address the issues both systematically—with long-term goals and objectives—and systemically—throughout all levels of our homes, schools and communities. There may be no immediate gratification, and we might not see the results we desire within our lifetimes. But that is not an excuse to delay our action.
- Read what your children read and watch what they watch. Listen to them. You won't have to do much prompting to elicit their feelings. They already have the questions *and* the nightmares. Ask them what they like about themselves. Ask yourself what you like about them. Write down the answers and read them out loud.

We now know a great deal about what is wrong with the world in which we are raising our children: that children who are abused become abusers; that children who are marginalized fail in school; that children who do not know how to resolve conflicts peacefully will do so violently. We need to be committed to learning as much about the solutions as we know about the problems, and then to do whatever we can to implement solutions.

If we listen well enough, children themselves will offer important and poignant advice:

To me, L.A. is a very special place. Some call it a melting pot, others a Third World city. L.A. is the home of modern multiculturalism, although some use the label as a good thing, while others use it as an insult. I like the diversity of this city. I thrive on it. You see, I'm biracial. Los Angeles has produced me, and countless other multiracial, multiethnic, multicultural children like me, who recognize the need for peace within ourselves and between our communities. If I must be a conduit for this process, so be it. I volunteer. And I hope that others, with the same sentiments as mine, will do the same. For you see, I owe it to my parents, my city and all the communities I am a part of, to do no less than rebuild our home.

And:

Parents cannot change the color of their children's eyes, but they can give their eyes the light of understanding and warmth of sympathy. They cannot alter their child's features, but they can, in many ways, help endow them with the glow of humaneness, kindness and friendliness.

Give of yourself. Give as much as you can. And you can always, always give something, even if it is only kindness! If everyone were to do this and not be as mean with a kindly word, then there would be much more justice and love in the world. Give and you shall receive much more than you would have ever thought possible. No one has ever become poor from giving!

The first quote is from a teenager in Los Angeles writing after the riots. The second is from Anne Frank, who died in a concentration camp during World War II.

It is our responsibility as parents, teachers, community leaders and friends of children everywhere to make sure that the fate of our children is that of the first child and not that of the second.

PRAYERS FOR PEACE

Baha'i

Be generous in prosperity, and thankful in adversity.

Be fair in thy judgment, and guarded in thy speech.

Be a lamp unto those who walk in darkness, and a home to the stranger.

Be eyes to the blind, and a guiding light unto the feet of the erring.

Be a breath of life to the body of humankind, a dew to the soil of the human heart, and a fruit upon the tree of humility.

Buddhist

May all beings everywhere plagued with sufferings of body and mind quickly be freed from their illnesses.

May those frightened cease to be afraid, and may those bound be free.

May the powerless find power, and may people think of be-
friending one another.

May those who find themselves in trackless, fearful wilder-
nesses—the children, the aged, the unprotected—be guarded
by beneficent celestials, and may they swiftly attain Buddha-
hood.

Christian

Blessed are the peacemakers, for they shall be known as the
Children of God. But I say to you that hear, love your enemies,
do good to those who hate you, bless those who curse you, pray
for those who abuse you. To those who strike you on the cheek,
offer the other also, and from those who take away your cloak,
do not withhold your coat as well. Give to everyone who begs
from you, and of those who take away your goods, do not ask
them again. And as you wish that others would do to you, do
so to them.

Hindu

Oh God, lead us from the unreal to the Real. Oh God, lead us
from darkness to light. Oh God, lead us from death to immor-
tality. Shanti, Shanti, Shanti unto all. Oh Lord God almighty,
may there be peace in celestial regions. May there be peace on
earth. May the waters be appeasing. May herbs be wholesome,
and may trees and plants bring peace to all. May all beneficent
beings bring peace to us. May thy Vedic Law propagate peace all
through the world. May all things be a source of peace to us.
And may thy peace itself bestow peace on all, and may that peace
come to me also.

Jainist

Peace and Universal Love is the essence of the Gospel preached by all the Enlightened Ones. The Lord has preached that equanimity is the Dharma. Forgive do I creatures all, and let all creatures forgive me. Unto all have I amity, and unto none enmity. Know that violence is the root cause of all miseries in the world. Violence, in fact, is the knot of bondage. "Do not injure any living being." This is the eternal, perennial, and unalterable way of spiritual life. A weapon, howsoever powerful it may be, can always be superseded by a superior one; but no weapon can, however, be superior to nonviolence and love.

Jewish

Come let us go up the mountain of the Lord, that we may walk the paths of the Most High. And we shall beat our swords into ploughshares, and our spears into pruning hooks. Nation shall not lift up sword against nation—neither shall they learn war any more. And none shall be afraid, for the mouth of the Lord of Hosts has spoken.

Muslim

In the name of Allah, the beneficent, the merciful. Praise be to the Lord of the Universe who has created us and made us into tribes and nations, that we may know each other, not that we may despise each other. If the enemy incline toward peace, do thou also incline toward peace, and trust in God, for the Lord is the one that heareth and knoweth all things. And the servants of God, Most Gracious, are those who walk on the Earth in humility, and when we address them, we say, "Peace."

Native American

O Great Spirit of our Ancestors, I raise my pipe to you. To your messengers the four winds, and to Mother Earth who provides for your children. Give us the wisdom to teach our children to love, to respect and to be kind to each other so that they may grow with peace in mind. Let us learn to share all the good things that you provide for us on this Earth.

Shinto

Although the people living across the ocean surrounding us, I believe, are all our brothers and sisters, why are there constant troubles in this world? Why do winds and waves rise in the ocean surrounding us? I only earnestly wish that the wind will soon puff away all the clouds which are hanging over the tops of the mountains.

Sikh

God adjudges us according to our deeds, not the coat that we wear: That Truth is above everything, but higher still is truthful living. Know that we attaineth God when we loveth, and only that victory endures in consequence of which no one is defeated.

Zoroastrian

We pray to God to eradicate all the misery in the world: that understanding triumph over ignorance, that generosity triumph over indifference, that trust triumph over contempt and that truth triumph over falsehood.

Resources

ADVERTISING & CONSUMER CONCERNS

American Advertising
  Federation
1400 K Street NW #100
Washington, DC 20005
(202) 898-0089

Badvertising Institute
25 Boyd Street #2
Portland, ME 04101
(207) 773-3275

Consumers Union
101 Truman Avenue
Yonkers, NY 10703
(914) 378-2000

Public Citizen
PO Box 19404
Washington, DC 20036
(202) 833-3000

Scenic America
216 Seventh Avenue SE
Washington, DC 20003
(202) 546-1100

U.S. Consumer Product Safety
  Commission
5401 Westbard Avenue
Bethesda, MD 20207
(800) 638-CPSC
(301) 492-8104 in MD

U.S. Federal Trade Commission
Advertising Practices
Sixth and Pennsylvania Avenue
  NW
Washington, DC 20580
(202) 326-3131

U.S. Public Interest Research
  Group (PIRG)
215 Pennsylvania Avenue SE
Washington, DC 20003
(202) 546-9707

BILINGUAL EDUCATION

ASPIRA Association
1112 16th Street NW #340
Washington, DC 20036
(202) 835-3600

ERIC Clearinghouse for
   Bilingual Education
8737 Colesville Road #900
Silver Spring, MD 20910
(800) 647-0123

Intercultural Development
   Research Association
5835 Callaghan Road #350
San Antonio, TX 78228
(512) 684-8180

National Association for
   Bilingual Education
810 First Street NE, Third Floor
Washington, DC 20002
(202) 898-1829

National Clearinghouse for
   Bilingual Education
1118 22nd Street NW #217
Washington, DC 20037
(800) 321-NCBE
(202) 467-0867

CENSORSHIP

American Civil Liberties Union
132 West 43rd Street
New York, NY 10036
(212) 944-9800

American Library Association
Office of Intellectual Freedom
50 East Huron Street
Chicago, IL 60611
(312) 944-6780

Focus on Family
801 Corporate Center Drive
Pomona, CA 91768
(714) 620-8500

National Coalition Against
  Censorship
2 West 64th Street
New York, NY 10023
(212) 724-1500

Parents' Music Resource Center
1500 Arlington Boulevard
Arlington, VA 22209
(703) 527-9466

People for the American Way
Freedom to Learn Project
2000 M Street NW
Washington, DC 20036
(800) 326-PFAW
(202) 467-4999 in DC

Student Press Law Center
1735 Eye Street NW
Washington, DC 20006-2402
(202) 466-5242

CRIME & VIOLENCE

Congressional Crime Caucus
SH-303 Hart Senate Office
  Building
Washington, DC 20510
(202) 224-4254

Clearinghouse on Family
  Violence Information
PO Box 1182
Washington, DC 20013
(703) 385-7565

Cult Awareness Network
  (CULTS)
2421 West Pratt Boulevard
  #1173
Chicago, IL 60645
(312) 267-7777

Justice Statistics Clearinghouse
Bureau of Justice Statistics
U.S. Department of Justice
Box 6000
Rockville, MD 20850
(800) 732-3277
(301) 251-5500 in MD

Juvenile Justice Clearinghouse
Box 6000
Rockville, MD 20850
(800) 638-8736

Kids Against Crime
PO Box 22004
San Bernardino, CA 92406
(714) 882-1344

National Crime Prevention
  Council
1700 K Street NW, Second
  Floor
Washington, DC 20006
(202) 466-NCPC

Police Foundation
1001 22nd Street NW #200
Washington, DC 20037
(202) 833-1460

EDUCATION

American Council on Education
1 Dupont Circle NW #800
Washington, DC 20036
(202) 939-9300

Education Research Information
  Clearinghouse (ERIC)
Office of Educational Research
  and Improvements
  Information Service
U.S. Department of Education
555 New Jersey Avenue NW
  #300
Washington, DC 20208-5641
(800) USE-ERIC
(202) 626-9854 in DC

ERIC Clearinghouse on Rural
  Education and Small Schools
Appalachia Educational
  Laboratory, Inc.
1031 Quarrier Street
Charleston, WV 25325-1348
(800) 624-9120
(800) 344-6646 in WV

ERIC Clearinghouse for Science,
  Mathematics, and
  Environmental Education
1200 Chambers Road, Third
  Floor
Columbus, OH 43212
(614) 292-6717

ERIC Clearinghouse for Social
  Studies/Social Science
  Education
Social Studies Development
  Center
2805 East Tenth Street # 120
Bloomington, IN 47405
(812) 855-3838

ERIC Clearinghouse on Tests,
  Measurement, and Evaluation
American Institutes for Research
3333 K Street NW
Washington, DC 20002-3893
(202) 342-5060

ERIC Clearinghouse on Urban
Education
Teachers College Columbia
University
Institute for Urban and Minority
Education
525 West 120th Street #303
New York, NY 10027-9998
(212) 678-3433

Global Alliance for
Transformational Education
PO Box 21
Grafton, VT 05146
(802) 843-2382

National Education Association
(N.E.A.)
1201 16th Street NW
Washington, DC 20036
(202) 822-7226

National Community Education
Association
3929 Old Lee Highway, Suite
91
Fairfax, VA 22030
(703) 359-8973

National School Boards
Association
Resource Center/Library
1680 Duke Street
Alexandria, VA 22314
(703) 838-6722

National Society for Internships
and Experimental Education
3509 Haworth Drive
Raleigh, NC 27609
(919) 787-3263

FAMILY

Administration for Children and
Families
U.S. Department of Health &
Human Services
370 L'Enfant Promenade SE
Washington, DC 20447
(202) 401-9275

Association of Child Advocates
PO Box 5873
Cleveland, OH 44101
(216) 881-2225

Children's Defense Fund
122 C Street
Washington, DC 20001
(202) 628-8787

Child Welfare League
440 First Street NW #310
Washington, DC 20001-2085
(202) 638-2952

Coalition on Human Needs
1000 Wisconsin Avenue NW
Washington, DC 20007
(202) 342-0726

Family Information Center
National Agricultural Library
10301 Baltimore Boulevard
 #304
Beltsville, MD 20705
(301) 504-5719

Family Resource Coalition
200 S. Michigan Ave., Suite
 1520
Chicago, IL 60604-2404
(312) 341-0900

House Select Committee on
 Children, Youth and Families
U.S. Congress
Washington, DC 20515
(202) 226-7660

International Child Resource
 Institute
1810 Hopkins Avenue
Berkeley, CA 94707
(415) 644-1000
Fax: (415) 845-1115

GUNS & WEAPONS

Bureau of Alcohol, Tobacco and
 Firearms
U.S. Department of Treasury
650 Massachusetts Avenue
Washington, DC 20226
(202) 927-7777

Handgun Control Inc.
1225 Eye Street NW
Room 1100
Washington, DC 20005
(202) 898-0792

National School Safety
 Association
Pepperdine University
4165 Thousand Oaks Boulevard
 #290
Westlake, CA 91362
(805) 373-9977

HUMAN RIGHTS

Amnesty USA
322 Eighth Ave.
New York, NY 10001
(212) 807-8400

Children of the Earth Coalition
PO Box 217
Newfane, VT 05345
(802) 365-7616
Fax: (802) 365-7798

Congressional Human Rights
  Caucus
H2-552 House Office Building
  Annex 2
Washington, DC 20515
(202) 226-4040

Human Rights Advocates
  International
230 Park Avenue #460
New York, NY 10169
(212) 986-5555

U.S. Department of State
Bureau of Human Rights and
  Humanitarian Affairs
2201 C Street NW
Washington, DC 20520
(202) 647-2126

PEACE

American Friends Service
  Committee
1501 Cherry St.
Philadelphia, PA 19102-1403

Cumberland Center for Justice
  and Peace
PO Box 857
Sewanee, TN 37375
(615) 598-5369

Educators for Social
  Responsibility
23 Garden Street
Cambridge, MA 02138
(617) 492-1764

Fellowship of Reconciliation
Box 271
Nyack, NY 10960

Peace Development Fund
PO Box 270
Amherst, MA 01007
(413) 256-8306

U.S. Institute for Peace
1550 M Street NW
Washington, DC 20005-1708
(202) 457-6063

War Resister's League
339 Lafayette St.
New York, NY 10012
(212) 228-0450

Young and Teen Peacemakers
37 Lebanon Street
Hamilton, NY 13346
(315) 824-4332

PREJUDICE & RACISM

American-Arab Anti-
Discrimination Committee
4201 Connecticut Avenue NW
#500
Washington, DC 20008
(202) 244-2990

Anti-Defamation League of B'nai
B'rith
823 United Nations Plaza
New York, NY 10017
(212) 490-2525

Asian-American Legal Defense
and Education Fund
99 Hudson Street
New York, NY 10013
(212) 966-5932

Congressional Black Caucus
H2-344 House Office Building
Annex 2
Washington, DC 20515
(202) 226-7790

Congressional Hispanic Caucus
H2-557 House Office Building
Annex 2
Washington, DC 20515
(202) 226-3430

League of United Latin
American Citizens
400 First Street NW #716
Washington, DC 20001
(202) 628-0717

National Association for the
Advancement of Colored
People/Youth and College
Division
4805 Mount Hope Drive
Baltimore, MD 21215-3297
(301) 358-8900

National Institute Against
Prejudice and Violence
31 South Greene Street
Baltimore, MD 21201
(301) 328-5170

National Urban League
Youth Services Department
500 East 62nd Street
New York, NY 10021
(212) 310-9000

Students and Youth Against
Racism
PO Box 1819
New York, NY 10159
(212) 741-0633

224

RESOURCES

U.S. Commission on Civil
Rights
Clearinghouse Division
1121 Vermont Avenue NW
Washington, DC 20425
(212) 376-8113

U.S. Department of Justice
Community Relations Service
5550 Friendship Boulevard
#330
Chevy Chase, MD 20815
(800) 347-4283

STUDENT RIGHTS

American Civil Liberties Union
(ACLU)
132 West 43rd Street
New York, NY 10036
(212) 944-9800

Family Rights and Privacy Office
U.S. Department of Education
400 Maryland Avenue SW
Washington, DC 20202
(202) 735-1807

American Student Council
Association
National Association of
Elementary School Principals
1516 Duke Street
Alexandria, VA 22314
(703) 684-3345

National Association of Student
Councils
National Association of
Secondary School Principals
Division of Student Activities
1904 Association Drive
Reston, VA 22091
(703) 860-0200

TELEVISION & MEDIA

Accuracy in Media
1275 K Street NW #1150
Washington, DC 20005
(202) 371-6710

Cable Television Information
  Center
PO Box 1205
Annandale, VA 22003
(703) 941-1770

Center for Investigative
  Reporting
530 Howard Street, Second
  Floor
San Francisco, CA 94105-3007
(415) 543-1200

Corporation for Public
  Broadcasting
901 E Street NW
Washington, DC 20004
(202) 879-9600

Fairness and Accuracy in
  Reporting
130 West 25th Street
New York, NY 10001
(212) 633-6700

Federal Communication
  Commission
Mass Media Bureau
1919 M Street NW
Washington, DC 20554
(202) 632-7048

National Association of
  Broadcasters
1771 N Street NW
Washington, DC 20036
(202) 429-5300

National Coalition on Television
  Violence
144 East End Avenue
New York, NY 10128
(212) 535-7275

National Council for Families &
  Television
3801 Barham Boulevard #300
Los Angeles, CA 90068
(213) 876-5959

Keywords

Whether you are searching through the card catalog at your local library or surfing the Internet, the following list of keywords and search terms will assist you in finding more information about the issues mentioned in *Teaching Peace*:

ability grouping
advocacy
affirmative action
Afrocentrism
aggression
antibias
anti-discrimination
at-risk
bias
bias in testing
bigotry
bilingual
cable television
cartoons
census
change
children and firearms
children's literature
citizenship education
class
comic books
commercials

compassion fatigue
compliance
conflict management
conflict resolution
content area materials
cross-cultural communication
cultural boundaries
cultural content
cultural diversity
cultural literacy
cultural relativism
cultural unity
culture
curriculum
demographics
desegregation
discrimination
diverse workforce
diversity
diversity management
diversity training
dominant culture

dropout prevention
early childhood development
education reform
educational practices
EEO
elementary education
English as a Second Language
equal educational opportunity
ESL
ethnic diversity
ethnic relations
ethnicity
ethnocentric
Eurocentrism
family structure
family values
gangs
gender
gender bias
gender equity
gender-fair teaching
gender neutral
gender issues
gender role socialization
geographic shifts
global education
global perspective
global studies
guns and children
gun control
hate crime
higher education
human interaction
human resources
human rights
immigrants
immigration

inclusion
integration
intercultural communication
intercultural education
interracial families
invisibility
juvenile fiction
language acquisition
learning styles
linguistic form
mass media
media literacy
mediation
middle school
migrant education
minorities
minority students
multicultural awareness
multicultural counseling
multicultural curriculum
multicultural education
multicultural literature
multicultural workforce
multiculturalism
multiethnic
multilingual
multiple intelligences
nature of prejudice
network television
news bias
nonsexist
nonviolence
parent involvement
parental discretion
peace education
peace studies
pedagogy

pluralism
political correctness
population trends
prejudice
preschool
prime time television
professional development
race
race bias
racial discrimination
racism
recruitment
reverse discrimination
role entrapment
school policy
school violence
second language acquisition
secondary education
segregation
self-esteem
sex bias
sexist
sex typing

sexual harassment
social action
social development
socioeconomic status
socialization
staff development
stereotyping
teacher education
teaching strategies
television and children
television programming
television research
textbooks
tracking
values
video game violence
video games and youth
violence
violence and youth
violence in television
violence in video games
war toys
women's studies

Bibliography

Abrams, Grace C., Fran C. Schmidt. *Peace Is in Our Hands: A Resource Unit for Teachers of Kindergarten and Grades 1 to 6*. The Jane Addams Peace Association, Philadelphia, PA, 1974.

————. *Learning Peace: A Resource Unit*. The Jane Addams Peace Association, Philadelphia, PA, 1972.

Adams, Paul, Leila Berg, Nan Berger, Michael Duane, A. S. Neill, Robert Ollendorff. *Children's Rights: Toward the Liberation of the Child*. Praeger Publishers, 1971.

Adler, David A. *The Number on My Grandfather's Arm*. UAHC Press, 1987.

Aldridge, Bob and Janet. *Children and Nonviolence*. Hope Publishing House, 1987.

America's Women of Color: Integrating Cultural Diversity Into Non–Sex-Biased Curricula (Secondary Curriculum Guide). Women's Educational Equity Act Program, U.S. Department of Education, 1982.

America's Women of Color: Integrating Cultural Diversity Into Non–Sex-Biased Curricula (Elementary Curriculum Guide). Women's Educational Equity Act Program, U.S. Department of Education, 1982.

Archer, Dane, Rosemary Gartner. *Violence and Crime in Cross-National Perspective*. Yale University Press, 1984.

Austin, Susan, Gail Meister. *Responding to Children at Risk: A Guide to Recent Reports*. Research for Better Schools, 1990.

Baker, Gwendolyn C. *Planning and Organizing for Multicultural Instruction*. Addison-Wesley Publishing Company, Inc., 1983.

Barlett, Donald L., James B. Steele. *America: What Went Wrong?* Andrews and McMeel, 1992.

Bell, Terrel H. *Morality and Citizenship Education: Whose Responsibility?* Research for Better Schools, 1976.

Berger, Arthur Asa. *Media U. S. A.: Process and Effect.* Longman Publishing, 1988.

Bernstein, Richard. *Dictatorship of Virtue: Multiculturalism and the Battle for America's Future.* Alfred A. Knopf, 1994.

Beyond PC: Toward A Politics of Understanding. Graywolf Press, 1992.

Bodinger-deUriarte, Cristina, Anthony R. Sancho. *Hate Crime: Sourcebook for Schools.* Research for Better Schools, 1992.

Boutros-Ghali, Boutros. *An Agenda for Peace.* United Nations, 1992.

Bowker, Andy. *Sisters in the Blood: The Education of Women in Native America.* WEEA Publishing Center, 1993.

Braided Lives. An Anthology of Multicultural American Writing. Minnesota Humanities Commission, 1991.

Break the Lies That Bind: Sexism in the Media. Center for Media Literacy, 1994.

Breines, Paul. *Tough Jews: Political Fantasies and the Moral Dilemma of American Jewry.* Basic Books, 1990.

Campbell, Patricia B. *Encouraging Girls in Math and Science—Working Together, Making Changes: Working In and Out of School to Encourage Girls in Math and Science.* WEEA Publishing Center, 1992.

———. *Encouraging Girls in Math and Science—Math, Science, and Your Daughter: What Can Parents Do?* WEEA Publishing Center, 1992.

———. *Encouraging Girls in Math and Science—Nothing Can Stop Us Now: Designing Effective Programs for Girls in Math, Science, and Engineering.* WEEA Publishing Center, 1992.

———. *Encouraging Girls in Math and Science—What Works and What Doesn't?: Ways to Evaluate Programs for Girls in Math, Science, and Engineering.* WEEA Publishing Center, 1992.

———. *The Hidden Discriminator: Sex and Race Bias in Educational Research.* WEEA Publishing Center, 1989.

Carlsson-Paige, Nancy, Diane F. Levin. *Who's Calling the Shots?: How to Respond Effectively to Children's Fascination with War Play and War Toys.* New Society Publishers, 1990.

Carrera, John Willshire. *Immigrant Students: Their Legal Right of Access to Public Schools.* The National Center for Immigrant Students, National Coalition of Advocates for Students, 1989.

Carter, Jimmy. *Talking Peace: A Vision for the Next Generation*. Dutton Children's Books, 1993.

Casse, Pierre. *Training for the Cross-Cultural Mind (A Handbook for Cross-Cultural Trainers and Consultants)*. SIETAR (Society for International Education, Training and Resources), 1980.

Chapman, Anne. *The Difference It Makes: A Resource Book on Gender for Educators*. National Association of Independent Schools, 1988.

Chatfield, Charles, Ruzanna llukhina, editors. *Peace Mir: An Anthology of Historic Alternatives to War*. Syracuse University Press, 1994.

Children's Express (Susan Goodwillie, editor). *Voices from the Future: Our Children Tell Us About Violence in America*. Crown Publishers, Inc., 1993.

Ch'maj, Betty E. M., editor. *Multicultural America: A Resource Book for Teachers of Humanities and American Studies*. University Press of America, 1993.

Civil Rights Compliance: An Update. Intercultural Development Research Association, 1988.

Coles, Robert. *The Call of Service: A Witness to Idealism*. Houghton-Mifflin Co., 1993.

————. *Times of Surrender: Selected Essays*. University of Iowa Press, 1988.

Comstock, Margaret. *Building Blocks for Peace: A Resource Unit for Kindergarten Teachers*. The Women's International League for Peace and Freedom, 1973.

Convention on the Rights of the Child, United Nations Department of Public Information, 1991.

Dennison, George. *The Lives of Children*. Addison-Wesley Publishing Co., 1969.

Derman-Sparks, Louise. *The A.B.C. Task Force. Anti-Bias Curriculum: Tools for Empowering Young Children*. National Association for the Education of Young Children, 1989.

Dewing, Martha. *Beyond T.V.: Activities for Using Video with Children*. ABC-CLIO, Inc., 1992.

Donaldson, Margaret. *Children's Minds*. Fontana Press, 1978.

Drew, Naomi. *Learning the Skills of Peacemaking: An Activity Guide for Elementary-Age Children on Communicating, Cooperating, and Resolving Conflict*. Jalmar Press, 1987.

D'Souza, Dinesh. *Illiberal Education: The Politics of Race and Sex on Campus*. The Free Press, division of Macmillan, 1991.

Dumond, Val. *The Elements of Nonsexist Usage: A Guide to Inclusive Spoken and Written English*. Prentice Hall Press, 1990.

Edelman, Marian Wright. *The Measure of Our Success: A Letter to My Children and Yours*. Harper Perennial, 1992.

Elder, Pamela, Mary Ann Carr. *Worldways: Bringing the World Into the Classroom*. Addison-Wesley Publishing Co., 1987.

Erickson, Tim. *Off & Running: The Computer Offline Activities Book*. Equals, Lawrence Hall of Science, 1986.

Erikson, Erik H. *Childhood and Society*. W.W. Norton and Co., 1963.

Fairchild, Halford H., Luis Ortiz-Franco, Don T. Nakanishi, Lenore A. Stiffarm, editors. *Discrimination and Prejudice. An Annotated Bibliography*. Westerfield Enterprises, Inc., 1992.

Fenton, Edwin. *The Relationship of Citizenship Education to Values Education*. Research for Better Schools, 1977.

Fenwick, J. James, principal writer. *Caught in the Middle: Educational Reform for Young Adolescents in California Public Schools*. Calfornia Department of Education, 1987.

Filipovic, Zlata. *Zlata's Diary: A Child's Life in Sarajevo*. Viking/Penguin Books, 1994.

Ford, Clyde W. *We Can All Get Along: 50 Steps You Can Take to Help End Racism at Home, at Work, in Your Community*. Dell Publishing, 1994.

Framework for Multicultural Arts Education, A. National Arts Education Research Center, 1989.

Freire, Paulo. *The Politics of Education: Culture, Power and Liberation*. Bergin and Garvey Publishers, 1985.

Garbarino, James, Nancy Dubrow, Kathleen Kostelny, Carole Pardo. *Children in Danger: Coping With the Consequences of Community Violence*. Jossey-Bass Inc., 1992.

Garbarino, James, Kathleen Kostelny, Nancy Dubrow. *No Place to Be a Child: Growing Up in a War Zone*. Lexington Books/D.C. Heath and Co., 1991.

Garbarino, James, Frances M. Stott, faculty of The Erickson Institute. *What Children Can Tell Us: Eliciting, Interpreting, and Evaluating Critical Information from Children*. Jossey-Bass Inc., 1992.

Gardner, Howard. *The Unschooled Mind: How Children Think and How Schools Should Teach*. Basic Books, 1991.

Gelfand, Donald E., Russell D. Lee. *Ethnic Conflicts and Power: A Cross-National Perspective*. John Wiley and Sons, 1973.

Gilligan, Carol. *In a Different Voice*. Harvard University Press, 1982.

Glock, Charles Y., Robert Wuthnow, Jane Allyn Piliavin, Metta Spencer. *Adolescent Prejudice*. Harper and Row, 1975.

Goldberg, Susan. *Times of War and Peace: Dealing with Kid's Concerns*. Annick Press, 1991.

Gonzalez-Mena, Janet. *Multicultural Issues in Child Care*. Mayfield Publishing Company, 1993.

Goodlad, John I. *A Place Called School*. McGraw-Hill Book Company, 1984.

Grant, Carl A., Christine E. Sleeter. *Turning on Learning: Five Approaches for Multicultural Teaching Plans for Race, Class, Gender, and Disability*. Macmillan Publishing, 1989.

Guide to Non-Sexist Children's Books, A: Volume II, 1976-1985. Academy Chicago Publishers, 1987.

Hart, Thomas E., Linda Lumsden. *Confronting Racism in the Schools*. Oregon School Study Council, 1989.

Hartoonian, H. Michael. *Rethinking Social Education: Ideas and Recommendations from Wingspread*. Wisconsin State Department of Public Instruction, 1983.

Helping Children Love Themselves and Others: A Professional Handbook for Family Day Care. The Children's Foundation, 1990.

Helping Children Love Themselves and Others: A Resource Guide to Equity Materials for Young Children. The Children's Foundation, 1990.

Henry, William A. III. *In Defense of Elitism*. Doubleday, 1994.

Hergert, Leslie F., Janet M. Phlegar, Marla E. Perez-Selles. *Kindle the Spark: An Action Guide for Schools Committed to the Success of Every Child*. The Regional Laboratory for Educational Improvement of the Northeast and Islands, 1991.

Herstory: A Simulation of Male and Female Roles Emphasizing the Amer-

ican Woman's Circumstances. Past and Present (Teacher Guide). Interaction Publishers, 1972.

Hewlett, Sylvia Ann. *When the Bough Breaks: The Cost of Neglecting Our Children*. HarperCollins Publishers, 1991.

Houston, Ronald A. *The Education of Minority Students in Non-Urban Schools*. Research for Better Schools, 1988.

How Schools Shortchange Girls: The AAUW Report. AAUW Educational Foundation and The National Education Association, 1992.

Hudson, Wade, Cheryl Willis Hudson, editors. *Black History Activity and Enrichment Handbook*. Just Us Books, Inc., 1990.

Hunter, James Davison. *Culture Wars: The Struggle to Define America*. Basic Books, 1991.

Intercultural Sourcebook (Cross-Cultural Training Methodologies). The Society for Intercultural Education, Training and Research, 1979.

Jhally, Sut, Justin Lewis. *Enlightened Racism: The Cosby Show, Audiences, and the Myth of the American Dream*. Westview Press, 1992.

Kammer, Ann E., Cherlyn S. Granrose, Jan B. Sloan. *Science, Sex, and Society: The Project for the Advancement of Women in Science Careers*. WEEA Publishing Center, 1979.

Karnow, Stanley, Nancy Yoshihara. *Asian Americans in Transition*. The Asia Society, 1992.

Kidron, Michael, Dan Smith. *The New State of War and Peace: An International Atlas*. Simon and Schuster, 1991.

Kilpatrick, William. *Why Johnny Can't Tell Right From Wrong, And What We Can Do About It*. Touchstone/Simon and Schuster, 1992.

Kohls, L. Robert, John M. Knight. *Developing Intercultural Awareness*. Intercultural Press, Inc., 1994.

Kolb, Frances Arick. *Portraits of Our Mothers: Using Oral History in the Classroom*. The Network, 1983.

Kozol, Jonathan. *The Night Is Dark and I Am Far From Home: A Bold Inquiry Into the Values and Goals of America's Schools* Simon and Schuster, 1975.

———. *Savage Inequalities*. Crown Publishers, 1991.

Kuipers, Barbara J. *American Indian Reference Books for Children and Young Adults*. Libraries Unlimited, 1991.

Levin, Diane E. *Teaching Young Children in Violent Times*. Educators for Social Responsibility, 1994.

Levin, Jack, Jack McDevitt. *Hate Crimes: The Rising Tide of Bigotry and Bloodshed.* Plenum Press, 1993.

Living in the Image Culture: An Introductory Primer for Media Literacy Education. Center for Media Literacy, 1992.

Lorenz, Konrad. *On Aggression.* Harcourt Brace and Co., 1963.

Lynch, James. *The Multicultural Curriculum.* Batsford Academic and Educational Ltd., 1983.

————. *Multicultural Education: Principles and Practice.* Routledge & Kegal Paul plc, 1986.

Macy, Joanna. *Despair and Personal Power in the Nuclear Age.* New Society Publishers, 1983.

Maslow, Abraham. *Motivation and Personality (2nd edition).* Harper and Row, 1954.

McDonald, Margaret Read. *Peace Tales: World Folktales to Talk About.* Linnet Books, 1992.

McGinnis, Kathleen, Barbara Oehlberg. *Starting Out Right: Nurturing Young Children as Peacemakers.* The Crossroad Publishing Co., 1991.

Meagher, Laura. *Teaching Children About Global Awareness.* The Crossroad Publishing Co. 1991.

Melaville, Atelia I., Martin J. Blank, Gelareh Asayesh. *Together We Can: A Guide to Crafting a Profamily System of Education and Human Services.* U.S. Department of Education, Office of Educational Research and Improvement, and U.S. Department of Health and Human Services, Office of the Assistant Secretary for Planning and Evaluation, 1993.

Menard, Sharon L. *How High the Sky? How Far the Moon?: An Educational Program for Girls and Women in Math and Science.* WEEA Publishing Center, 1979.

Meyrowitz, Joshua. *No Sense of Place: The Impact of Electronic Media on Social Behavior.* Oxford University Press, 1985.

Miles, Rosalind. *The Women's History of the World.* Salem House, 1989.

Miller, Alice. *For Your Own Good: Hidden Cruelty in Child-Rearing and the Roots of Violence.* The Noonday Press, division of Farrar, Straus and Giroux, 1990.

————. *Thou Shalt Not Be Aware: Society's Betrayal of the Child.* New American Library, 1984.

Miller-Lachmann, Lyn. *Our Family, Our Friends, Our World: An Anno-*

tated Guide to Significant Multicultural Books for Children and Teen-agers. R.R. Bowker, 1992.

Mindset for Math, A: Techniques for Identifying and Working with Math-Anxious Girls. The Ohio State University, 1987.

Montalto, Nicholas V. *A History of the Intercultural Education Movement, 1924–1941.* Garland Publishing, Inc., 1982.

Nickel, James W. *Making Sense of Human Rights: Philosophical Reflections on the Universal Declaration of Human Rights.* University of California Press, 1987.

Olson, Mancur. *The Logic of Collective Action: Public Goods and the Theory of Groups.* Harvard University Press, 1971.

On Prejudice: A Global Perspective. Anchor Books, 1993.

Parenting in a TV Age. Center for Media and Values, 1991.

Pasternak, Michael G. *Helping Kids Learn Multi-Cultural Concepts.* Research Press Company, 1979.

Peace, Roger C. III. *A Just and Lasting Peace: The U.S. Peace Movement from the Cold War to Desert Storm.* The Noble Press, 1991.

Pedersen, Paul, John C. Carey, editors. *Multicultural Counseling in Schools.* Allyn and Bacon, 1994.

Powell, Margaret H. *School/Community Relations: Freedom for Individual Development.* Wisconsin Department of Public Instruction, 1978.

Prothrow-Stith, Deborah. *Deadly Consequences: How Violence Is Destroying Our Teenage Population and a Plan to Begin Solving the Problem.* HarperPerennial, 1991.

Racism and Sexism in Children's Books: Interracial Digest #1. Council on Interracial Books for Children, 1976.

Ralph, John M., Christine Dwyer. *Making the Case: Evidence of Program Effectiveness in Schools and Classrooms—Criteria and Guidelines for the U.S. Department of Education's Program Effectiveness Panel.* U.S. Department of Education, 1988.

Ramsey, Patricia G. *Multicultural Education.* Garland Reference Library of Social Science (Volume 355), 1989.

Reardon, Betty A. *Comprehensive Peace Education: Educating for Global Responsibility.* Teachers College Press, 1988.

Reed, Ishmael, Kathryn Trueblood, Shawn Wong. *The Before Columbus Foundation Fiction Anthology.* W. W. Norton and Co., 1992.

Reiss, Alabert J., Jr., Jeffrey A. Roth, editors. *Understanding and Preventing Violence*. National Academy Press, 1993.

Renyi, Judith. *Going Public: Schooling for a Diverse Democracy*. The New Press, 1993.

Rosenblatt, Roger. *Children of War*. Anchor Press, 1983.

Rufus, Anneli. *The World Holiday Book: Celebrations for Every Day of the Year*. HarperSanFrancisco, 1994.

Rushdie, Salman. *Haroun and the Sea of Stories*. Penguin Books, 1990.

Russell, Diana E. H. *Lives of Courage: Women for a New South Africa*. Virago Press, 1990.

Rutstein, Nathan. *Healing Racism in America: A Prescription for the Disease*. Whitcomb Publishing, 1993.

Sadker, Myra, David Sadker. *Failing at Fairness: How America's Schools Cheat Girls*. Charles Scribner's Sons, 1994.

Saracho, Olivia N., Bernard Spodek, editors. *Understanding the Multicultural Experience in Early Childhood Education*. NAEYC (National Association for the Education of Young Children), 1983.

Schaef, Ann Wilson. *Women's Reality: An Emerging Female System in a White Male Society*. Harper Paperbacks, 1981.

Schlesinger, Arthur M., Jr. *The Disuniting of America: Reflections on a Multicultural Society*. Whittle Direct Books, 1991.

Schmidt, Fran, Alice Friedman. *Creative Conflict Solving for Kids (2nd edition)*. Peace Education Foundation, 1985.

Schmidt, Fran, Alice Friedman, Jean Marvel. *Mediation for Kids: Kids in Dispute Settlement*. Grace Contrino Abrams Peace Education Foundation, 1992.

Schmidt, Fran, Alice Friedman, Elyse Brunt, Theresa Solotoff. *Peace-Making Skills for Little Kids (Activity Book)*. Peace Education Foundation, 1992.

Schmidt, Fran, Alice Friedman. *Creative Conflict Solving for Kids (1st edition)*. Grace Contrino Abrams Peace Education Foundation, 1991.

Schrumpf, Fred, Donna Crawford, H. Chu Usadel. *Peer Mediation: Conflict Resolution in Schools (Program Guide)*. Research Press Company, 1991.

Schuman, Jo Miles. *Art From Many Hands: Multicultural Art Projects*. Davis Publication, 1981.

Screening Educational Equity: A Filmography. The Mid-Atlantic Equity Center, 1989.

Seely, Robert. *The Handbook of Non-Violence.* Lawrence Hill and Co., Westport, CN and Lakeville Press, 1986.

Senge, Peter M. *The Fifth Discipline: The Art and Practice of The Learning Organization.* Doubleday, 1990.

Shaffer, Carolyn R., Kristin Anundsen. *Creating Community Anywhere: Finding Support and Connection in a Fragmented World.* Jeremy P. Tarcher/Perigee Books, 1993.

Singer, Linda R. *Settling Disputes: Conflict Resolution in Business, Families, and the Legal System.* Westview Press, 1990.

Slapin, Beverly, Doris Seale, Rosemary Gonzalez. *How to Tell the Difference: A Checklist for Evaluating Children's Books for Anti-Indian Bias.* New Society Publishers, 1992.

Smey-Richman, Barbara. *Involvement in Learning for Low-Achieving Students.* Research for Better Schools, 1988.

———. *School Climate and Restructuring for Low-Achieving Students.* Research for Better Schools, 1991.

———. *Teacher Expectations and Low-Achieving Students.* Research for Better Schools, 1989.

Smith, Mary Ann, Joan Kalvelage, Patricia A. Schmuck. *Sex Equity in Educational Leadership: Women Getting Together and Getting Ahead.* WEEA Publishing Center, 1982.

Stewart, Edward C., Milton J. Bennett. *American Cultural Patterns: A Cross-Cultural Perspective.* Intercultural Press, Inc., 1991.

Subject Headings and Classification on Peace and International Conflict Resolution (Guides to Library of Congress). United States Institute of Peace, 1990.

Takaki, Ronald. *A Different Mirror: A History of Multicultural America.* Little, Brown and Company, 1993.

Tannen, Deborah. *You Just Don't Understand: Women and Men in Conversation.* Ballentine Books, 1990.

Taylor, Jared. *Paved With Good Intentions: The Failure of Race Relations in Contemporary America.* Carroll and Graf Publishers, 1992.

Terkel, Studs. *Race.* The New Press, 1992.

Terry, Robert W. *For Whites Only.* William B. Eerdmans Publishing Co., 1970.

Thompson, W. Scott, Kenneth M. Jensen, editors. *Approaches to Peace: An Intellectual Map*. United States Institute of Peace, 1992.

Tiedt, Pamela L., Iris M. Tiedt. *Multicultural Teaching: A Handbook of Activities, Information, and Resources*. Allyn and Bacon, Inc., 1979.

Toffler, Alvin. *The Third Wave*. Bantam Books, 1980.

Toffler, Alvin, Heidi Toffler. *War and Anti-War: Survival at the Dawn of the 21st Century*. Little, Brown and Co., 1993.

Tutu, Desmond. *Hope and Suffering*. William B. Eerdmans Publishing Co., 1984.

TV Alert: A Wake-Up Guide for Television Literacy. Center for Media Literacy, Walsh, Roger. *Staying Alive: The Psychology of Human Survival*. New Science Library, 1984.

Wheelock, Anne. *Crossing the Tracks: How "Untracking" Can Save America's Schools*. The New Press, 1992.

When Hate Groups Come to Town: A Handbook of Effective Community Responses. The Center for Democratic Renewal, 1992.

Van Ornum, William, Mary Wicker Van Ornum. *Talking to Children About Nuclear War*. The Continuum Publishing Co., 1984.

Volkan, Vamik D. *The Need to Have Enemies and Allies: From Clinical Practice to International Relationships*. Jason Aronson, Inc., 1988.

For information on workshops and lectures based on the material in this book, or to offer comments and suggestions for future editions, please write to . . .

Jan Arnow
Institute for Intercultural Understanding
3020 Bardstown Road, #199
Louisville, Kentucky 40205

. . . send an e-mail message to:

jarnow@iglou.com

. . . or see my homepage on the World Wide Web:

http://iglou.com/members/jarnow